W9-CDI-058

ARTIFICIAL INTELLIGENCE

▲ by Kathryn Hulick

Content Consultant

Asa Ben-Hur
Associate Professor of Computer Science
Colorado State University

Essential Library

An Imprint of Abdo Publishing | abdopublishing.com

CUTTING EDGE
SCIENCE +
TECHNOLOGY

abdopublishing.com

Published by Abdo Publishing, a division of ABDO, PO Box 398166, Minneapolis, Minnesota 55439. Copyright © 2016 by Abdo Consulting Group, Inc. International copyrights reserved in all countries. No part of this book may be reproduced in any form without written permission from the publisher. Essential Library™ is a trademark and logo of Abdo Publishing.

Printed in the United States of America, North Mankato, Minnesota
092015
012016

THIS BOOK CONTAINS
RECYCLED MATERIALS

Cover Photo: Shutterstock Images

Interior Photos: Seth Wenig/AP Images, 4–5; Red Line Editorial, 7, 17, 29, 51; Jared Lazarus/Feature Photo Service/IBM/AP Images, 9; Kathy Willens/AP Images, 11; US Navy, 13; iStockphoto, 14–15, 25, 31, 36–37, 44; Ingo Wagner/Picture-Alliance/DPA/AP Images, 19; James Looker/PC Gamer Magazine/Getty Images, 21; Franck Boston/Shutterstock Images, 22; Jeon Heon-Kyun/EPA/Newscom, 26–27; Shutterstock Images, 31, 78–79; Brian Lawless/Press Association/AP Images, 35; Tony Avelar/AP Images, 39; Heritage Images/Corbis, 41; Ted S. Warren/AP Images, 46; Matt Sayles/Invision for Microsoft/AP Images, 48–49; Barone Firenze/Shutterstock Images, 53; Chris Ratcliffe/Bloomberg/Getty Images, 55; Steve Lagreca/Shutterstock Images, 56–57; Art Konovalov/Shutterstock Images, 59; Google/Rex Features/AP Images, 60; Damian Dovarganes/AP Images, 63; Julian Stratenschulte/Picture-Alliance/DPA/AP Images, 65; Kyodo/AP Images, 66–67; Craig Barritt/Getty Images, 69; Matt Rourke/AP Images, 71; J. Scott Applewhite/AP Images, 73; Peter Cihelka/The Free Lance-Star/AP Images, 75; DARPA/AP Images, 77; Haruyoshi Yamaguchi/Corbis, 81; Rick Friedman/Corbis, 83; Sam Ogden/Science Source, 85; Shizuo Kambayashi/AP Images, 86; The Painting Fool/www.thepaintingfool.com/Prof. Simon Colton at Falmouth University and Goldsmiths College, London, 89; Alan Siu/EyePress EPN/Newscom, 90–91; Hubert Boesl/Picture-Alliance/DPA/AP Images, 93; George Frey/Getty Images, 96; Michael Bahlo/Picture-Alliance/DPA/AP Images, 99

Editor: Nick Rebman
Series Designer: Craig Hinton

Library of Congress Control Number: 2015945645

Cataloging-in-Publication Data

Hulick, Kathryn.
 Artificial intelligence / Kathryn Hulick.
  p. cm. -- (Cutting-edge science and technology)
ISBN 978-1-62403-912-6 (lib. bdg.)
Includes bibliographical references and index.
1. Artificial intelligence--Juvenile literature. I. Title.
006.3--dc23

2015945645

CONTENTS

ONE

COMPUTER
CHAMPIONS

Three game show contestants stood by their buzzers, ready to play *Jeopardy!* But something was unusual in this episode—one of the players was not human. A computer screen perched in between two men wearing suits. The display showed a picture of a glowing planet Earth. This was Watson.

Game show host Alex Trebek walked out onto the set. "You are about to witness what may prove to be an historic competition," he said to the audience. "An exhibition match pitting an IBM computer system against the two most celebrated and successful players in *Jeopardy!* history."[1]

Watson had some tough competition. Ken Jennings held the record for the most *Jeopardy!* victories with a 74-game winning streak. Brad Rutter had won more than $3 million on the show—more than any other contestant.[2] Could a computer defeat these two trivia experts?

Watson, center, plays Jeopardy! against human champions Ken Jennings, left, and Brad Rutter, right.

Watson does not have a squishy, pinkish-gray brain made of cells and neurons. Instead, its intelligence comes from a room full of whirring machinery: 750 powerful computer servers linked in a high-speed network, cooled by large refrigerator units. The servers provide 15 terabytes of memory and the computing power of 2,800 regular computers.[3]

During the *Jeopardy!* game, Watson was not linked to the Internet. Instead, it accessed millions of pages of research material loaded onto its servers: books, movie scripts, encyclopedias, and more. How could Watson possibly get an answer wrong with so much information at its disposal? The tricky part for Watson was not recalling trivia—it was understanding the clues.

Learning Natural Language

Anyone who has ever tried to learn a new language knows words can be tricky. Some words and phrases mean more than one thing. For example, consider these two sentences: "An athlete runs on a track" and "A car runs on gas." The meanings of *run* and *on* are different in each sentence. After all, the car is not scampering across a pool of gas. It is very difficult to teach a computer which meaning applies in any particular sentence.

Scientists who work on artificial intelligence (AI) refer to the sentences people speak every day as "natural language." Typically, computers follow instructions in programming languages, which are written in code. In these computer languages, the words must be very precise. Each word or symbol means one thing. But most people do not know how to write code. Therefore, a computer that can understand natural language makes communication between people and machines easier and more straightforward for everyone.

Trivia Time!

In the game of *Jeopardy!*, players are told the answers, and each response must be in the form of a question. Here are some samples from Watson's appearance on the show. The top row gives the categories, and the bottom row gives the answers. Can you beat the computer by figuring out the questions?

NAME THE DECADE	LITERARY CHARACTER APB	ALTERNATE MEANINGS	ALSO ON YOUR COMPUTER KEYS	FINAL FRONTIERS
DISNEYLAND OPENS & THE PEACE SYMBOL IS CREATED	HIS VICTIMS INCLUDE CHARITY BURBAGE, MAD EYE MOODY & SEVERUS SNAPE; HE'D BE EASIER TO CATCH IF YOU'D JUST NAME HIM!	A PIECE OF WOOD FROM A TREE, OR TO PUNCTURE WITH SOMETHING POINTED	IT'S AN ABBREVIATION FOR GRAND PRIX AUTO RACING	TICKETS AREN'T NEEDED FOR THIS "EVENT," A BLACK HOLE'S BOUNDARY FROM WHICH MATTER CAN'T ESCAPE

Correct response:
What are the 1950s?

Watson:
Unsure

Correct response:
Who is Voldemort?

Watson:
Unsure

Correct response:
What is a stick?

Watson:
Correct

Correct response:
What is F1?

Watson:
Unsure

Correct response:
What is an event horizon?

Watson:
Correct

Where Is Watson Now?

Watson can do much more than compete on a quiz show. Now, the same AI technology that played on *Jeopardy!* helps doctors treat patients. New medical information comes out every day, and it is impossible for doctors to read and learn about every new discovery. They need an easy way to search all that data. The system ClinicalKey uses Watson's DeepQA technology to search thousands of medical journals, textbooks, and reports. With this type of technology, a future with robot doctors is possible.

Imagine walking up to a computer, telling it your symptoms, and then finding out what's wrong and what the best treatment is—all in natural language.

IBM's Watson technology also helped write a cookbook, *Cognitive Cooking with Chef Watson*. IBM and the Institute of Culinary Education gave Watson a database of online recipes, nutritional facts, and flavor research. Then the supercomputer came up with entirely new dishes, including Italian-pumpkin cheesecake.

The technology company IBM spent three years working on an AI technology, called DeepQA, that could answer natural language questions quickly and correctly. The goal was to match or even beat human performance. They chose *Jeopardy!* as a test because the show uses natural language, covers many different topics, requires answers in less than three seconds, and has penalties for wrong answers. Watson used the DeepQA technology to answer questions during the quiz show appearance.

With each clue, Watson used more than 100 different techniques to understand the clue, decide how to search for answers, and rank all the possible answers. Each answer gets a confidence score that measures how likely it is to be correct. To prepare for the show, Watson trained hard, working through more than 100,000 sample *Jeopardy!* questions.[4] When it made a mistake, the IBM team could teach Watson how to handle that type of clue.

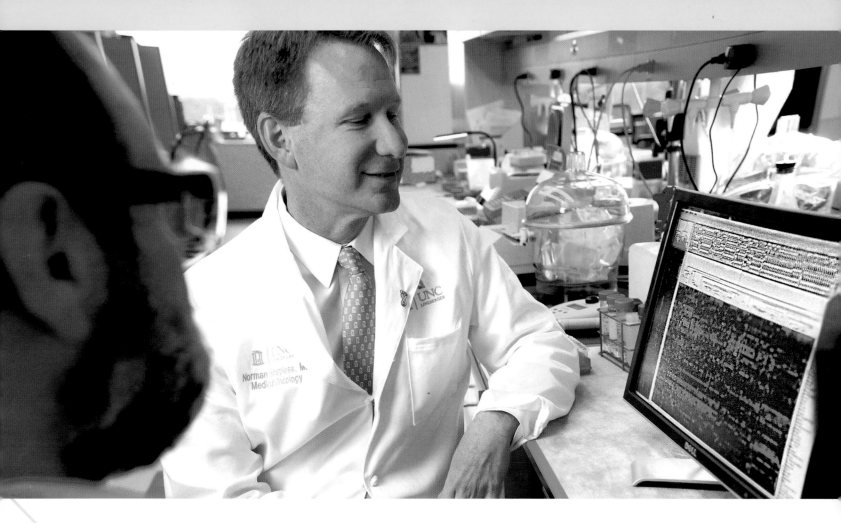

Doctors began using Watson to help determine treatment options for cancer patients.

This *Jeopardy!* match took place in February 2011 over two days. Jennings and Rutter got lots of right answers, but not enough to beat Watson. The computer won easily with a final score of $77,147—more than the two humans' scores combined.[5]

Artificial Champions

Watson was neither the first nor the last computer program to defeat a human opponent. The checkers program Chinook was the first to win a human championship in 1994. Three years later, an IBM program named Deep Blue defeated Garry Kasparov, the world's chess champion. In 2015, a group of computer scientists in Canada announced a computer program named Cepheus, which plays an essentially perfect game of poker.

Chinook, Deep Blue, Watson, and Cepheus are each examples of AI. AI shows up in many cutting-edge technologies, including robots, driverless cars, web searches, and video games. AI technologies use sophisticated algorithms, or sets of instructions, to solve a variety of difficult problems.

In science fiction, AI characters are typically robots with superhuman brains. In reality, scientists still cannot build a robot that learns, sees, listens, talks, walks, interacts, and reasons as well as a person. Instead, there are many different technologies that

Garry Kasparov, left, plays chess against Deep Blue in 1997. Feng-Hsiung Hsu, one of Deep Blue's designers, moves the pieces for the computer.

Poker Face

Unlike chess, poker is a game that involves chance and hidden, or imperfect, information. Players keep their cards secret and make bets on who has the best hand. Players can bluff, or pretend to have good cards when they don't. They can also fold, or quit a round, if they think their cards cannot win. In 2015, a team of Canadian researchers announced that their computer program Cepheus could play a certain style of poker better than any human. To come up with its winning strategy, Cepheus played billions of games against itself, putting in a total of 1,000 years of practice. This practice time was spread out across a cluster of 5,000 computers.[8]

accomplish just one or two of those tasks. For example, Watson is excellent at answering questions. Siri, the personal assistant on the iPhone, can understand what a person says. The PackBot, produced by the company iRobot, excels at navigating through unfamiliar terrain. Other AI technologies work behind the scenes to figure out who and what people like while they are using social media or shopping online. And some AIs—such as Watson and Deep Blue—become world champions!

The PackBot is being used by explosives technicians in the US military.

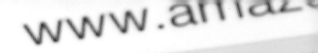

Try Prime

Shop by Department ▾

Unlimited Instant V̶

MP3s & Cloud Player
20 million songs, play anywhere

Amazon Cloud Drive

TWO

DEEP LEARNING

When a human is born, he or she does not know how to do much of anything. Things people do easily every day, such as tying their shoes or reading, take years of practice. Many AI technologies practice and learn, too. Watson trained with thousands of sample *Jeopardy!* questions before competing on the show. Machine learning happens when a program changes itself so it can perform better in the future. Deep learning is a new breakthrough in AI that helps a program recognize general patterns in a way that is somewhat similar to how human brains work.

Not all computer programs can learn. Some simply follow precise instructions for everything they do. For example, a calculator can add, subtract, divide, and multiply, but it will never figure out how to calculate the areas of shapes unless a programmer adds specific instructions. However, many programs and apps that people use every day incorporate machine learning.

Companies such as Amazon.com use AI to better understand what their customers might be interested in buying.

When Internet users buy products on Amazon.com, watch movies on Netflix, or listen to music on Spotify, recommendation systems try to figure out users' interests to suggest things they might like. These recommendations change based on each user's browsing and purchase history and any ratings he or she provides. Amazon.com also groups together people with similar interests and uses all of their data to make better recommendations to the group. The more a person uses any of these services, the better the recommendations get. Users' actions train the AI to better understand what they like.

Inspired by the Brain

Computer scientists have come up with many different approaches to help computers learn, but the most promising technology today is called deep learning. It is based on the concept of neural networks. The human brain is a neural network with approximately 100 billion neurons linked with 100 trillion connections.[1] Information goes into a person's brain from his or her senses; then neurons process that information and generate output that the person experiences as thoughts, feelings, and physical responses. Artificial neural networks (ANNs) take

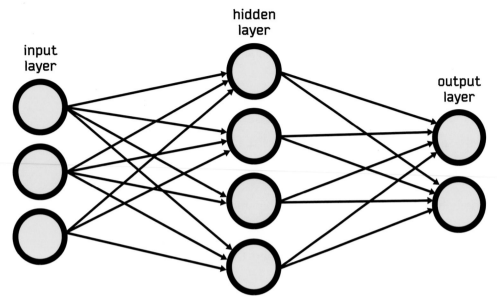

Neural Network

In this diagram, each dot represents an artificial neuron, and each line represents a connection between two neurons. Information is processed in the hidden layer.

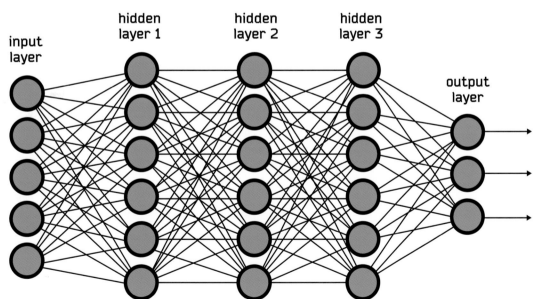

Deep Neural Network

In deep learning, there are many more neurons, in multiple layers, with many more connections between them.

data such as images, text, or spoken words as their input, and they output helpful information about the data.

The biggest ANNs in AI today have more than a billion connections.[2] These giant networks can process huge amounts of data—all at the same time—to find patterns. These patterns combine together into higher and higher levels of meaning.

For example, to recognize a photograph of a face, an ANN first has to identify every pixel of an image and how it relates to the pixels around it. At this level, the program recognizes concepts such as light or dark. Patterns found at this level get passed up to the next level, where the program determines that certain arrangements of light and dark indicate an edge. Now the edges get passed up through more levels, which learn to find shapes including eyes and noses. Yet another level will learn to find two eyes above one nose and one mouth. Eventually, the final level compares the whole face to similar faces of people the program has seen in the past.

Marvin Minsky of the Massachusetts Institute of Technology (MIT) built the first neural network simulator in 1951. In the 1980s, Yann LeCun, who is now head of the Artificial Intelligence Research Lab at Facebook, developed new programming techniques for neural networks. He created a system that learned to recognize handwriting on checks, and many banks still use variants of that system today. Neural networks were a popular choice for solving learning problems through the 1990s. However, by the early 2000s, many AI researchers had moved on to other machine learning methods they viewed as more practical.

But in 2006, Geoffrey Hinton of the University of Toronto came up with a new approach he called "deep learning." His approach tweaked how the neurons are connected to each other in a way that provides better results more quickly. The word *deep* refers to the number of layers in the network. More

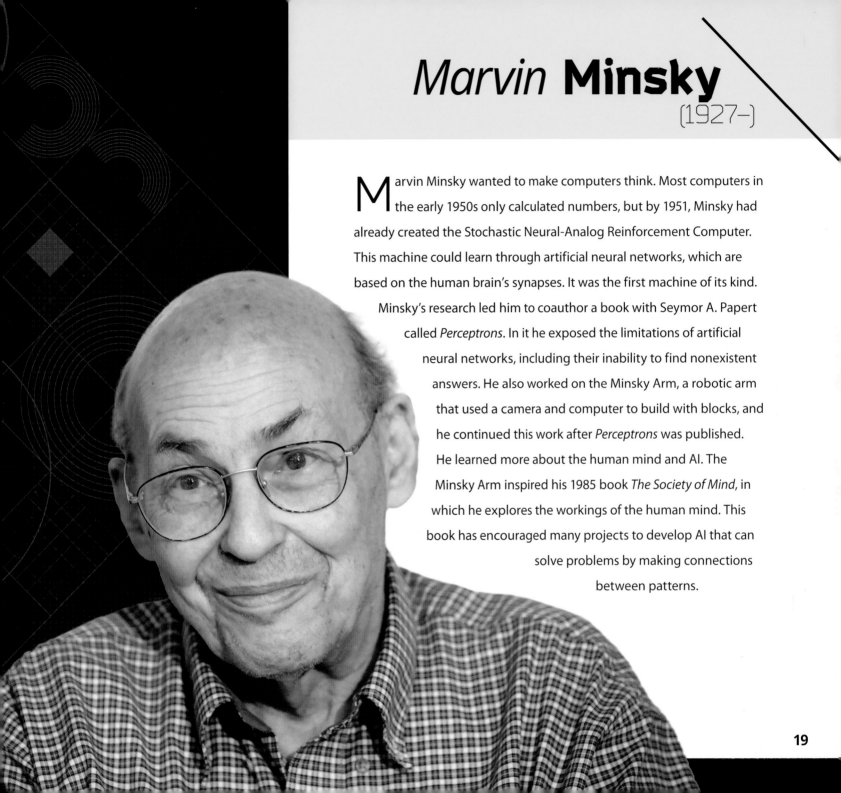

Marvin **Minsky**
(1927–)

Marvin Minsky wanted to make computers think. Most computers in the early 1950s only calculated numbers, but by 1951, Minsky had already created the Stochastic Neural-Analog Reinforcement Computer. This machine could learn through artificial neural networks, which are based on the human brain's synapses. It was the first machine of its kind. Minsky's research led him to coauthor a book with Seymor A. Papert called *Perceptrons*. In it he exposed the limitations of artificial neural networks, including their inability to find nonexistent answers. He also worked on the Minsky Arm, a robotic arm that used a camera and computer to build with blocks, and he continued this work after *Perceptrons* was published. He learned more about the human mind and AI. The Minsky Arm inspired his 1985 book *The Society of Mind*, in which he explores the workings of the human mind. This book has encouraged many projects to develop AI that can solve problems by making connections between patterns.

19

Drug Discovery

Discovering new drugs takes an enormous amount of work. First, researchers have to identify a specific reaction inside the body as a target. This might be a reaction that reduces pain or causes some other healing effect. Then, they have to search through data about chemicals to find one that will cause the same reaction but will not lead to bad side effects. Drug companies have plenty of data about the targets and the chemicals, but matching them up is time-consuming and difficult.

In 2012, the company Merck sponsored a challenge to researchers to match up chemicals with targets. A team of Geoffrey Hinton's students at the University of Toronto won the first prize of $22,000 with a deep learning program.[3] None of the humans had experience in medicine or drug research, but that did not matter. The AI still managed to defeat the other machine learning programs in the competition.

layers mean the program can recognize higher levels of patterns in the data. Hinton and his students are still developing the technique; in 2012, they won a contest to identify potential new drugs—even though none of them had studied medicine. A deep learning program sorted through the data, which contained descriptions of thousands of different molecules.

Deep learning got even faster with the invention of a new kind of computer chip called a graphics processing unit (GPU). This chip could perform parallel processing, meaning it could process multiple sets of instructions at the same time. Initially, this chip was made to handle the visuals in fast-paced video games. But in 2009, Andrew Ng of Stanford University started using these chips in neural networks. Before the GPU, most computers could process only one thing at a time, and it would take several weeks to make sense of the connections in a neural network. Now, the same computation can happen in a day, and neural networks can handle billions of connections. More connections mean more complexity in a neural network, which results in smarter AI technology.

"We want to take AI . . . to wonderful new places," said Hinton, "where no person, no student, no program has gone before."[4]

Learning in the Wild

All neural networks need training in order to improve. This training typically involves repeating a task over and over, with feedback that lets the program know whether it got the right answer. During

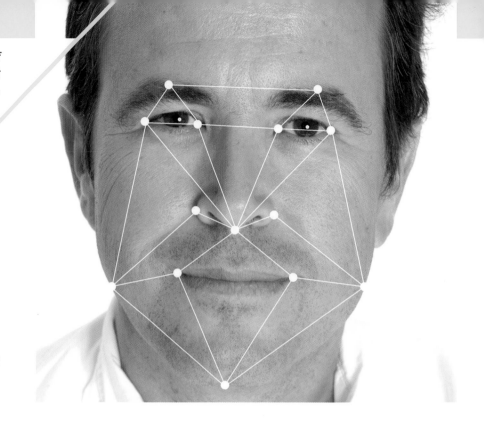

Facial recognition software analyzes a number of different points on a person's face to determine that person's identity.

"supervised learning," programmers train the AI with concrete examples of the task they want it to perform. For example, the programmers might show the AI pictures of frogs, each labeled with the word *frog*. Then, they show the AI entirely new photos, and the AI must identify the frogs. This is similar to learning in a classroom with a teacher standing over students' shoulders and pointing out the answers again and again until they can do the task on their own.

But machine learning can also be unsupervised, meaning the AI adapts to a new situation on its own—"in the wild," as some programmers describe it.[5] Imagine a person is stranded on a desert island, and she comes across a spiky yellow fruit she has never seen before. She would quickly learn to recognize this fruit, even without anyone telling her what it is. She might not know the fruit's name, but that does not matter. She would notice a pattern and realize the spiky yellow things growing on trees belong in the same category.

Some deep networks start out unsupervised, like the person stranded on the island. Once they have built up a set of patterns they recognize, the programmers then provide concrete examples.

The Google Brain project demonstrated successful unsupervised learning in 2012. The researchers gave the AI images from 10 million YouTube videos, but the AI received no labels or other identifying information. After three days, the program had defined several categories: human faces, human bodies, and cats. When Google applied this new technology to its Android assistant—an AI that listens and responds to speech—errors dropped by 25 percent.[6] This was one of the first applications of deep learning in a consumer product, and other companies took note.

Researchers at companies including IBM, Facebook, Microsoft, and others are creating ever-larger networks and developing even better deep learning algorithms. The technology has been applied to many different areas of AI: IBM created Watson, Facebook can identify family and friends in users' photos, and Microsoft improved language translation. In the next few years, websites, devices, robots, and even cars will become more and more intelligent thanks to deep learning.

GOOGLE BREAKTHROUGHS
FROM YOUTUBE TO ATARI

AI programs enjoy cat movies and video games as much as anybody. Andrew Ng of Stanford University started the Google Brain project in 2011. A year later, the team had built a deep learning neural network with one billion connections that learned to detect cats. The AI had no idea what a cat was beforehand. Instead, it learned the way a human child would. It noticed patterns in the way cats looked and decided they all must be the same kind of thing. So the program created a feature detector—a part of its programming that recognizes and responds to images of cats.

Google made another breakthrough in unsupervised learning in 2014 after acquiring the company DeepMind. This team developed an algorithm called Deep-Q Network (DQN). They tested the algorithm's ability to recognize patterns and build on past experiences with a series of Atari video games.

The same AI played 49 games including *Video Pinball*, *Breakout*, and *Space Invaders*.[7] It did not know any of the rules. All it had to work with were the images on the screen, the goal of getting a high score, and its ability to learn. DQN did not master all of the games, but it scored better than a human video game tester on more than half of them.

"It's learned to play all of these games with superhuman performance," said Google CEO Larry Page. "We've not been able to do things like this with computers before."[8] Deep learning made the AI smart enough to figure out the games on its own.

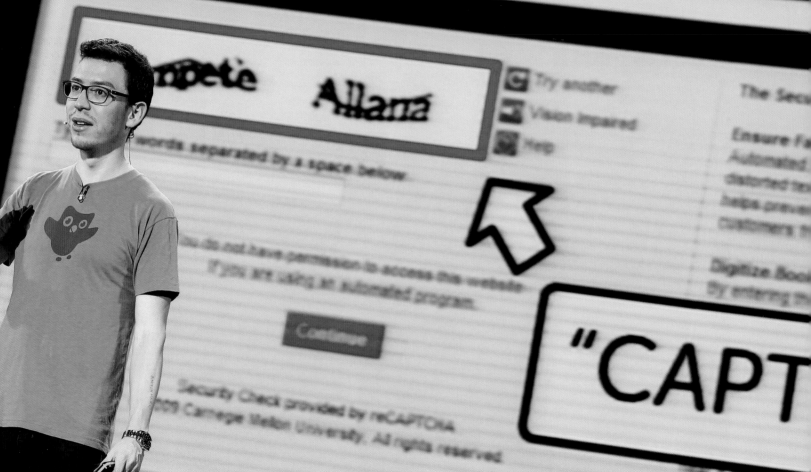

THREE

GOT THE PICTURE?

If a person looks at thousands of photos of cats and dogs, she can probably figure out which animal is which every time. For example, a small fluffy dog might look similar to some cats, but a human will not have much trouble identifying it as a dog. People do a great job at visual tasks such as this one, but it is a tricky problem for a computer. Cats and dogs stand in many different positions. They come in all different shapes, sizes, and colors.

Humans also prove their visual superiority every time they complete a form on a website asking them to identify a string of fuzzy, crooked, or slanted numbers and letters. This type of test is called a CAPTCHA, or Completely Automated Public Turing Test to Tell Computers and Humans Apart. This test is intended to prove a user is human and not a program, called a bot, trying to hack a website. CAPTCHA tests work because people are good at recognizing distorted text, and most bots are not.

Luis von Ahn, an entrepreneur and computer science professor, discusses CAPTCHAs at a conference in 2014.

But this is changing. In fact, the latest AI technology from Google can now identify even extremely distorted text with 99.8 percent accuracy.[1] Since the old CAPTCHA cannot trick computers any more, Google invented a new kind of test involving a graphic that changes from a spinning circle to a check box. Humans interact with the graphic differently from bots. The system may also show the user an image-matching problem or a picture of distorted text as an additional step.

A Competition for Computers

Computers are also learning to see cats, dogs, and other objects. At the ImageNet Large Scale Visual Recognition Challenge, computer programs look at pictures and identify objects such as cats, dogs, airplanes, bananas, and violins. In 2012, Geoffrey Hinton won the competition with a deep learning program. The next year, every entry in the competition used deep learning. Then, in 2014, a team of Microsoft researchers built a program that beat an average human's performance for the first time. People tend to make mistakes on 5.1 percent of the images.

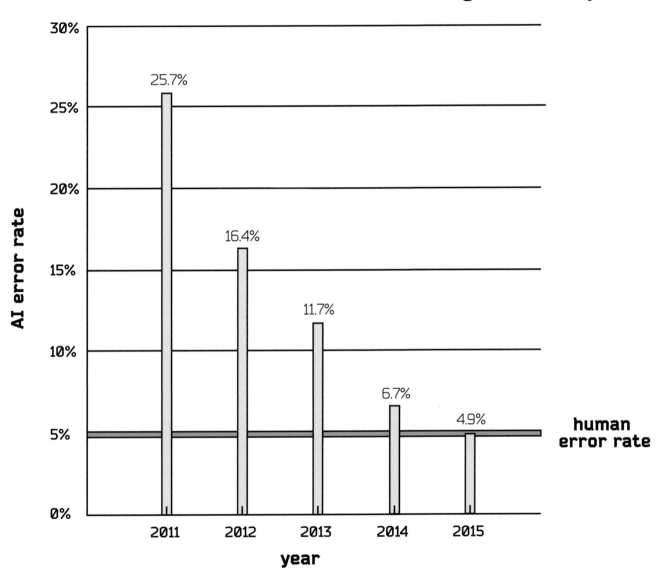

Microsoft's deep learning system achieved a 4.94 percent error rate.[3] Soon after the 2014 competition, Google researchers matched this error rate with their own deep learning program.

ImageNet is a collection of more than 14 million images from Flickr and other online photo sources.[4] People have located and labeled the objects within each image. Before the contest each year, teams of researchers get a set of 50,000 training images tagged with 1,000 different categories.[5] Similar to a student studying flash cards before a test, the AI must learn from these pictures. During training, the AI might see several photos featuring a breed of dog—for example, a Great Dane. The Great Danes would be in different positions and against different backgrounds, with labels identifying them all as Great Danes. Then, during the contest, the AI will get a totally new set of images with their labels missing. One image might show a Great Dane, while the next might show a motorcycle or a cactus. The AI must identify the objects in each picture.

Although AI can now beat humans in this particular contest, computer vision still is not perfect. And it is very different from human vision. For example, it is easier for a computer to identify the small differences between hundreds of different types of dogs than to identify the broader categories of dog and cat.

In addition to helping computers understand categories of objects, researchers have also started teaching computers how to describe the action in an image. For example, is the Great Dane running, jumping, or eating? In late 2014, two separate groups of researchers, one at Stanford University and one at Google, each developed AI programs that can write captions for images. The programs trained on images that humans had described; then the programs applied captions to totally new images. The technology is not perfect. To describe a picture of a baby with a toothbrush, Stanford's program wrote,

Cat Captions

The training image on the left includes a picture and a caption. The AI figures out how the words in the caption match up with the picture. Finally, the computer is able to create new descriptions for a similar image.

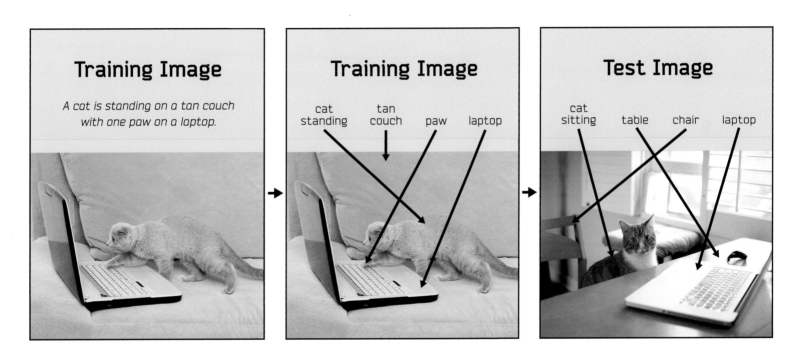

Training Image

A cat is standing on a tan couch with one paw on a laptop.

Training Image

cat standing   tan couch   paw   laptop

Test Image

cat sitting   table   chair   laptop

"A young boy is holding a baseball bat."[6] But the majority of the captions make sense. Again, neural networks and deep learning made the breakthrough possible.

◢ Superstars

Computer scientists who are working on facial recognition often use a set of training images called Labeled Faces in the Wild (LFW). It is a set of 13,000 pictures of more than 5,000 different celebrities—from Kelly Clarkson to Leonardo DiCaprio to Bill Clinton—each labeled with the person's name.[9] The images are available for free online to help train or test AI programs.

When the average person looks at two unfamiliar faces in this data set, he can tell if they are photos of the same person 97.53 percent of the time. DeepFace reached nearly the same accuracy, at 97.35 percent.[10] A research team in China developed an AI program that beat human performance and achieved 98.52 percent accuracy on the same set of images.[11]

DeepFace

People help train AI technology every time they add photos to Facebook. Facebook has more than 1.3 billion active users, and those users upload 400 million new photos every day.[7] Many people tag these photos with their friends' and family members' names. Every tagged photo is an image that can help make Facebook's AI better. In 2015, Facebook researchers announced their DeepFace software could identify faces as well as a human. The program used a nine-layer deep neural network with 120 million connections.[8]

Computers have been able to find faces in photos for a long time. After all, every face has eyes, a nose, and a mouth in a similar arrangement. Identifying specific individuals is a much more difficult problem. A person's face is constantly changing: when she smiles, all of her features move. She could stand in a dark room or hang upside-down, yet her friends would still know who she was. A computer might get tricked. Computer scientists sum up these problems with the nickname A-PIE, which stands for Aging, Pose, Illumination, and Expression. All of these factors cause a picture of a person's face to change so much that a computer might think she is a different person.

Smart Selfies

Today, most mobile devices and computers come with cameras. Researchers are working on AI technology that can use these cameras to determine whether people are feeling happy, angry, sad, or bored. They train the AI using videos of people showing a wide variety of emotions. The AI can even detect microexpressions, which are tiny facial movements not noticeable to most people.

Right now, companies are using this technology to test people's reactions to ads before releasing them.

But in the future, a company might ask for access to a user's smartphone camera in order to automatically suggest movies, books, or other products based on the user's reactions to ads. Another research group at the University of Rochester wants to help track mental health. Their AI looks at more than expressions. It also reads heart rate based on changes in skin color; in addition, it tracks the user's Twitter posts and other online activity.

One reason DeepFace did so well is that it can rotate faces to compare them facing forward. It does this by fitting the features from a 2-D picture of a face onto a 3-D model. It uses these 3-D models to compare the features that are visible in each 2-D picture. Another reason for the success of DeepFace is the huge amount of data it had to practice with. Facebook users give the company permission to use their images when they sign up. Therefore, the researchers had access to a library of 4.4 million tagged Facebook photos to train their AI.[12] And the more an AI program trains, the more accurate it gets.

DeepFace is still a research project, but it has a lot of potential in the real world. The Federal Bureau of Investigation (FBI) is already using software to try to identify criminals from photos, but their system is not as accurate. Advertisers are also working on facial recognition and analyzing facial expressions. If they could detect how people feel, they could use built-in cameras in laptops, phones, and other devices to watch consumers and better target them with ads and products they might like.

Catching Bad Guys

Fingerprints are not the only way to catch a criminal. A person's face is even easier to recognize. But what can a law enforcement agency do when it has a picture but no name? The FBI can now turn to the Next Generation Identification (NGI) system. It still includes fingerprint data, but it also holds millions of faces linked to names. Many are mug shots of criminals, but other pictures come from regular people who went through background checks while applying for jobs.

When looking for a match, the FBI's system is not as accurate as the most cutting-edge AI. If a match exists, NGI will find it approximately 85 percent of the time.[13] But over time, this system and similar ones will get better and better, and many people worry about privacy. They want to know how their photos will end up in the system, and they want the government to ask permission before storing personal information. A group of concerned citizens wrote a letter to the government explaining the database could be used to watch or track innocent Americans. They asked the FBI to remove all images of noncriminals from the database.

AI technology that can see and understand images is already helping robots and driverless cars find their way around. Neurosurgeons are using computer vision and instrument tracking to perform safer surgeries. This technology helps people analyze and sort through a wide variety of visual information, from personal photos to scientific data.

Police departments are using facial recognition software to identify suspects.

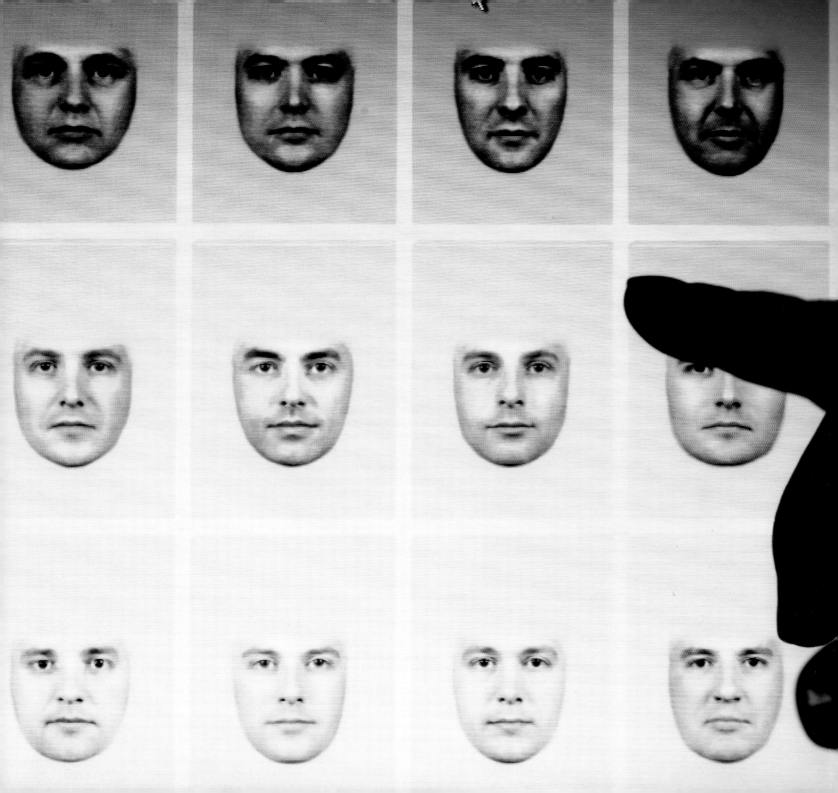

What can I help you with?

FOUR

TALKING WITH
MACHINES

Siri, a virtual assistant, is a form of AI that millions of people interact with every day. Several different technological feats are happening at the same time when a human has a conversation with Siri. First, Siri has to detect the person's speech and correctly figure out what words he is saying. This process is called speech recognition. Then, Siri has to understand those words and answer the person. This requires natural language processing. Finally, Siri connects to apps and services on the person's device to perform the task or provide the information he requested.

Siri first appeared in 2010 as an independent app for Apple's iPhone. Three weeks later, Siri's developers got a personal call from Steve Jobs, who was the head of Apple. Apple bought the company and made Siri an integral part of its new products. Since then, AI technology for detecting, understanding, and generating speech has continued to improve, and other

Early versions of Siri had trouble understanding certain accents, such as those from southerners.

companies are developing personal assistants similar to Siri.

But natural language remains a tricky problem. Knowing the meanings of words is not enough—computers also need common sense. To explain the problem, Marvin Minsky of MIT used the example of a piece of string. String can be used to tie a knot, drag a toy, or fly a kite, but it cannot be used to cut paper or hammer a nail. "In a few minutes," wrote Minsky, "any young child could tell you a hundred ways to use a string—or not to use a string—but no computer knows any of this. The same is true for ten thousand other common words."[1] To really comprehend language, a computer needs a pile of practical knowledge about the world.

Students work on drones at Singularity University, an institution founded by Ray Kurzweil.

At Google, AI expert Ray Kurzweil is working on the natural language problem. His goal is to develop AI technology that understands and uses language even more fluidly than IBM's Watson. Most people think of Google as merely a way to search the web. However, the algorithm Google uses is cutting-edge AI technology, and it is getting better every day. In 2012, Google introduced the Knowledge Graph, a service that can provide answers to search questions in place of links. The Knowledge Graph contains 700 million topics, including people, locations, and the relationships among these things.[2]

The Defense Advanced Research Projects Agency (DARPA), which is a part of the US Department of Defense, has funded research and competitions that led to driverless cars and more advanced robotics. In 2015, the agency announced the Communicating with Computers (CwC) program, which aims to develop AI that can easily process natural language and work collaboratively with humans.

The Turing Test

The idea of having a conversation with a machine goes back to Alan Turing, a British mathematician whose ideas formed the basis of modern computer science. In an essay published in 1950, he posed the question, "Can machines think?"[4] In an attempt to answer this question, he proposed a game that has become known as the Turing Test. In this game, a person has two conversations using typed messages. One conversation is with a human, and the other is with a computer—but the person does not know which is which. For the computer to pass the test, it must fool more than 30 percent of observers into thinking it is human. Turing believed computers would be able to pass this test by the year 2000. He said, "One will be able to speak of machines thinking without expecting to be contradicted."[5]

Turing's prediction was off by only a few years. In 2014, a computer program posing as a 13-year-old Ukrainian boy passed the Turing Test. In a series of five-minute conversations, 33 percent of the judges believed the AI program, named Eugene Goostman, was human.[6] But Eugene certainly did not understand the conversation on the same level that a person would. And some observers did not agree Eugene had truly passed the test, as the programmers used clever tricks to get around the difficulty of handling natural language. For example, Eugene was asked, "Did you see the Jubilee?" He responded, "Try to guess! Actually, I don't understand why you are interested. I know you are supposed to trick me."[7] That could be the answer to almost any question Eugene did not understand.

Alan **Turing**
(1912–1954)

Alan Turing described the modern computer in 1936, long before the technology to build one existed. He imagined a machine, now known as a "universal Turing machine," that contained a ribbon-like piece of tape that went on forever.[8] The tape gave the machine a way to remember instructions. It could read symbols written on the tape, or erase old symbols or write new ones.

This machine was just a mathematical idea, but it describes modern computer programming. The tape is a computer's memory, and the symbols are the ones and zeros of binary code that store information. A series of these symbols makes up a computer program.

At the time, machines were created for a specific purpose. An engineer might build a machine to add numbers together, or a machine to calculate taxes. Turing's machine could solve any logical problem; it just needed the right instructions.

Turing died tragically at the age of 41, two years after being convicted of indecency because he was gay. The United Kingdom pardoned him in 2013, nearly 60 years after his death.

Speech Recognition

The Turing Test does not require a machine to listen to spoken language or talk. But typing or tapping out commands does not make sense in today's world. People are starting to expect that phones, cars, music players, and other devices will hear humans' voices—and talk back. Many experts believe we are on the verge of an Internet of Things, or a network of everyday objects such as phones, cars, and even thermostats or parking spaces that all have the ability to connect and converse. "Speech is an enabling technology for the Internet of Things," said Andrew Ng, who started working on speech recognition for the Chinese search engine Baidu in 2014.[9]

Speech recognition has improved dramatically since 2009, when Geoffrey Hinton and his student George Dahl were the first to apply deep learning techniques to the problem. In 2014, Ng's team at Baidu developed a Deep Speech system that outperformed the latest technology from Google, Microsoft, and Apple. In noisy environments, the Baidu system correctly transcribed 81 percent of speech while the other systems were 65 percent accurate at best.[10]

According to Ng, two advances made these breakthroughs possible. One is the increased speed of computers that rely on GPUs for parallel processing. The team trained the Deep Speech AI on

100,000 hours of recorded speech—and processing such a huge amount of data requires a lot of computing power.[12] The other advance was deep learning.

A computer does not have ears, so it experiences speech as an audio wave form, which is a way of representing the sounds of words as a continuous stream of data. Early speech recognition technology looked at this wave form and tried to match the shapes of the sounds to the shapes of words stored in its dictionary. The problem with this approach is that everyone's voice sounds different, and even the same speaker may pronounce the same word differently depending on the sentence. For example, at the end of a question, the pitch of a word goes up. With deep learning, however, programmers do not have to worry about these variations. To train the program, they only have to provide numerous examples of spoken speech along with the words that are being said. The program figures out the patterns on its own.

Tim Tuttle works for Expect Labs, a company that is creating a system to add voice commands to mobile apps. He predicted that computers will soon be better at understanding speech than people are. "We're going to live in a world where devices don't have keyboards," he said.[13]

How to Speak Chinese Instantly

Speech recognition and language processing technologies can do much more than help people play music or get directions. They can also help people communicate with each other. Rick Rashid, head of Microsoft Research, gave a talk on machine learning at a conference in Tianjin, China, in 2012. Rashid did not know Chinese, but toward the end of the talk, a computerized voice that sounded just like him

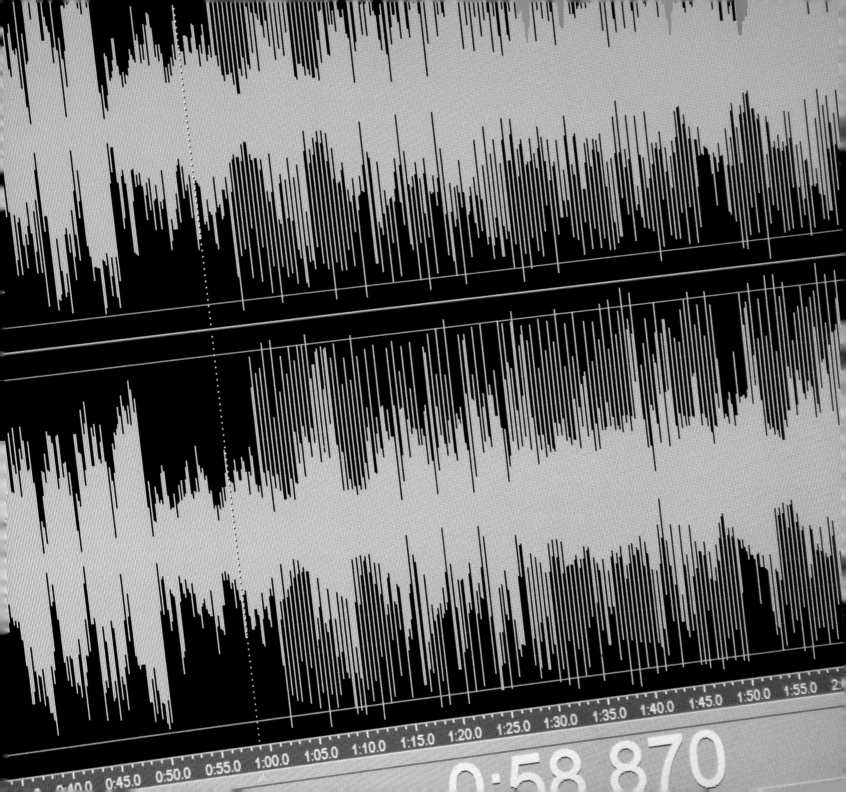

started giving his speech in that language. The audience broke out in applause. This demonstration led to the creation of Skype Translator, a new technology from Microsoft.

Real-time translation involves all the same hurdles as speech recognition and language processing, plus the challenge of figuring out words and phrases in a new language. The Microsoft system that became Skype Translator first converts speech to text. Next, it uses text-to-text translation to convert each word to the other language. Then, the system rearranges the words to fit the grammar of the second language.

Finally, Skype Translator can convert text back to speech in a new language. The system even produces speech that sounds like the original speaker's voice. To achieve this, Rashid explained, the Microsoft team took an hour-long recording of his voice plus a few hours of a person speaking Chinese. The system used data about Rashid's voice to change the Chinese speech so it sounded like him.

At the end of his presentation, Rashid said, in both English and Chinese, "The results are not perfect. . . . There's much work to be done in this area. But this technology is very promising, and we hope in a few

◢ Just Like *Star Trek*

Before Microsoft debuted the technology behind Skype Translator, speech-to-speech translation had existed only in science fiction. In *Star Trek*, for example, the crew have universal translators that allow them to speak with alien civilizations.

Every day, automatic text-to-text translation helps millions of people read web pages written in other languages. But translating speech to speech is a much more difficult problem—and it cannot use the same technology, because people do not talk the same way they write. Text translators usually rely on punctuation, but speech does not contain any helpful commas or periods. When people speak, they often use words such as *um* and *like* to fill spaces; they also repeat words or pause in the middle of a thought. An AI that translates speech must be able to filter out these extra words and sounds to focus on the meaning of users' sentences.

Skype Translator enables users to see translated text and hear translated audio.

years that we'll be able to break down the language barriers between people. Personally I believe this is going to lead to a better world."[14]

A preview version of Skype Translator became available to the public in late 2014. Although the voice sounded robotic and the translations often contained errors, every conversation helped the AI improve.

FIVE

VIDEO GAMES

People who play video games sometimes notice bugs, or places where the game acts strangely. Perhaps a chicken walks into a wall and gets stuck, or a zombie does not fight back while the gamer attacks it. These moments can ruin the experience of a game. However, AI programming can give characters ways to interact with their virtual world—and with the gamer. If the AI is working, the gamer should not notice any bizarre behavior.

Even though it is important for game AI not to mess up, it is not really important for the AI to be as smart as possible. While technologies such as Watson and Siri strive to surpass human abilities and make life more efficient with their super intelligence, the goal of a video game is to provide a player with a fun and engaging experience. Games also have to run quickly on systems that do not have a lot of memory to spare. A complicated AI system would eat up too much processing power. For those reasons, the cutting edge of game AI has not changed much since the early 2000s, and games

Gamers play an early version of
Halo 5 in 2014.

use AI techniques only when it makes sense to do so. Mainstream games do not feature deep learning. However, game programmers find plenty of other interesting approaches to creating lifelike game characters.

Sense, Think, Act

Game AI follows a cycle of sense, think, and act. First, non-player characters (NPCs) must experience their world—they need to see and hear the things around them. If a bomb explodes near a giant spider, the spider needs to realize it happened. Then, it must make decisions based on what is going on; it should want to run away from the explosion. Finally, it has to act on its decision and actually scamper off. A game may also add the ability to learn or remember from an experience. However, NPCs often do not live long enough for learning to serve any practical purpose.

The heart of game AI is in how these characters decide what to do. Several different programming techniques offer ways to organize and implement NPC behavior. One is called a finite state machine. This approach includes a series of states—such as search, fight, and run away—and the transitions between those states. The combat cycle of most fighting games can be pictured as a finite state machine: an enemy starts out searching for someone—the gamer. When

◢ Fun or Brains?

NPCs have access to perfect information about the game world instantly. If programmers made them as smart as possible, they could easily beat the gamer every time. A game such as *Halo* would not be much fun if the enemies could see through walls, or if they always aimed perfectly with every shot. Making a game fun often means building flaws into the AI on purpose. Damian Isla, a game AI programmer who worked on the *Halo* series, explained: "A lot of the time, we actually program deliberate mistakes into the AI to give the player a chance to do something as a reaction."[1] The player's experience of the game is what matters.

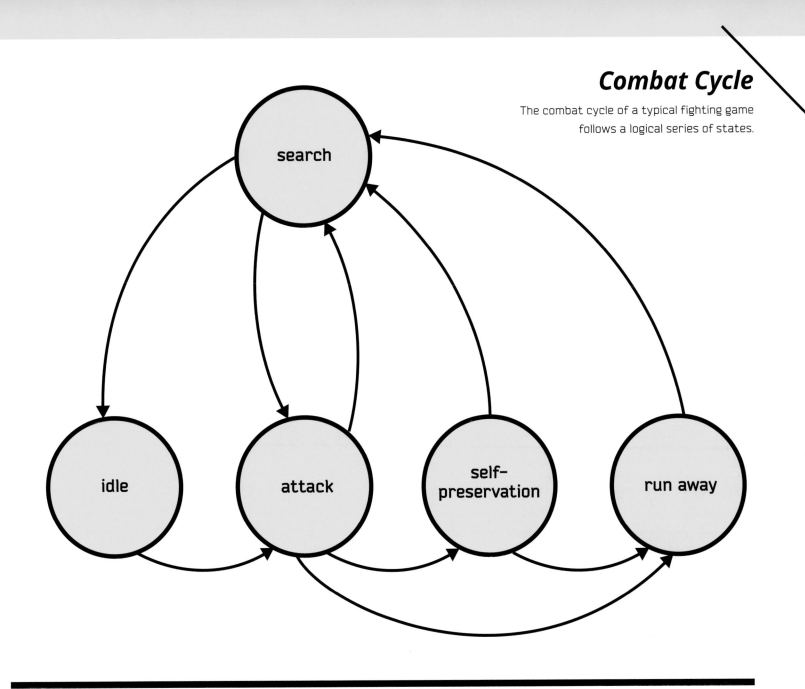

Combat Cycle

The combat cycle of a typical fighting game follows a logical series of states.

the enemy sees the gamer, he attacks. If the enemy's health drops too low, he runs away. This cycle can also include states such as idle, for when there is nothing for the enemy to do, and self-preservation, which may involve ducking or hiding.

A behavior tree is another popular AI technique. It is a series of lists of actions that get sorted by priority. At the highest level are broad actions such as search, combat, and fleeing. Once the AI has selected which of those makes sense given the situation, the action breaks down into a new list of subactions. For example, if the AI determines that a wolf NPC needs to attack, the behavior tree provides a new list of priorities to choose from in order to make that behavior happen. These attack options may include biting, lunging, and stalking. Behavior trees form the AI architecture of many popular games, including the *Halo* series.

Navigating the Mesh

One of the most difficult problems in game AI is also one of the easiest parts of the game for most players: walking from one place to another. Programmers call this problem pathfinding, and it is tricky because the NPC usually cannot follow a line directly from one point to another. Objects such as trees, rocks, or buildings get in the way. The NPC cannot "see" these obstacles. Instead, it relies on a map that represents the world as a grid, or mesh. In 3-D games, the mesh is formed from triangles that

Gamers play Dance Central *while the Microsoft Kinect tracks their movements.*

approximate the shapes of objects in the world. Some of the triangles can be navigated (such as a road or a meadow), and others cannot (such as a boulder or a wall). The NPC has to perform a series of searches to find a path along the triangle mesh that will get it to its destination without getting stuck or walking in circles.

Infinite Dungeons

The game world itself may be a product of an AI technology known as procedural generation. This technique creates game levels or content automatically. For example, each time a gamer plays

Minecraft, the world is different. And every time a gamer explores a dungeon in any of the *Diablo* games, the shape of the maze changes, presenting the player with new arrangements of rooms, enemies, and treasures. In contrast, the levels in a game such as *Super Mario 3D World* are exactly the same every time they are played.

It is even possible to procedurally generate entire games. Michael Cook built an AI program named Angelina to do just that while he was a student at Imperial College in London. Some of the games are similar to *Super Mario Bros.*, where the player jumps from platform to platform looking for the exit. Others are 3-D mazes the player can explore.

Michael Cook built Angelina for his PhD project. First, he provided Angelina with some rules describing what a good video game looks like and how it works. Then, Angelina combined random game components together—art, music, and level design—and evaluated the results to see if they made a good game. The more games Angelina makes, the less random the choices get. Cook said, "The system is intelligently selecting good ones with good traits. Over time it gets more and more focused."[2] With time, AI technology could help create new and exciting game ideas in addition to the characters and worlds it already helps build.

Minecraft has sold more than 60 million copies worldwide.

SIX

DRIVERLESS CARS

Flying cars may still be in the realm of science fiction, but intelligent cars have arrived. Google's driverless car has traveled more than 1 million miles (1.6 million km) on regular roads.[1] The cars have gotten into a few minor accidents, but these were all caused by human error, not the AI. Google is still testing its futuristic vehicle, but many new cars already come with AI technology. Some cars park themselves; others accelerate and brake to keep pace with traffic. Some can even tell if a driver seems drowsy or is not paying attention.

The 2013 Ford Explorer came with a camera that scans the road ahead and finds the lane markers. The Driver Alert system then figures out where the car should be on the road. If the vehicle starts to drift, the system chimes and flashes a warning to the driver.

Mercedes–Benz also offers Attention Assist technology, which monitors steering, braking, and acceleration to

Automaker Mercedes-Benz unveiled a self-driving concept car in 2015. The front seats can turn around, enabling all passengers to face each other.

Smart Parking

Automatic parking technology can already help guide a car into a parallel parking space without any mistakes or frustration. The company Valeo is taking parking tech to the next level with its Valet Park4U system. With this system, a driver can pull up to a parking lot, get out of the vehicle, and start automatic parking from a smartphone app. The car drives through the lot by itself to find a space, and it returns to the entrance when the driver calls for it. The cameras that guide the car also watch out for people or animals and can stop the car if needed.

create a model of how the driver usually behaves. When this behavior changes, an alert goes off.

Adaptive cruise control (ACC) uses either radar or cameras to track a vehicle traveling in front of it on a road. ACC then automatically slows down or speeds up to stay within a set distance. As of 2013, 19 major automakers offered cars with this smart technology.[2] Cars with ACC also typically come with systems that detect when a crash is about to occur and take action to avoid it.

In 2010, Volvo introduced the first automotive vision system that could tell the difference between people and other objects such as trees or mailboxes. The researchers who developed this technology drove a combined 1 million miles (1.6 million km) testing and training the AI.[3] When the system sees a pedestrian, it warns the driver and then stops the car if the driver does not respond. Now, many cars come with vision systems that can see and identify pedestrians, cyclists, and other types of obstacles day or night. Mobileye Vision Technologies is working on an automatic driving system that can maneuver a car down freeways and through intersections. Audi is already testing it in its A7.

All of these systems require a human driver. Google, however, wants to take the driver out of driving.

Carmaker Tesla announced a feature called Autopilot in 2014. This feature enables Tesla cars to travel on highways without the driver touching the wheel.

The Google Car

When Google started developing driverless cars in the late 2000s, the company hired engineers who had worked on the DARPA challenges, a series of races for robot cars. Google's team added cameras and sensors to regular cars, including the Toyota Prius and Lexus 450h. Human drivers rode along and could take over from the computer if necessary. In 2014, Google started making its own driverless cars, designed for city driving, with a maximum speed of 25 miles per hour (40 kmh).[4]

Google designed its self-driving cars to have a cute, friendly look.

The original design for these cars had no steering wheel or brake pedal—just one button to start or stop. But California laws required that a human being must be able to take control in an emergency. The final prototype had controls for a human driver, but it certainly did not need them. The car's cameras and sensors could see at a distance of more than two football fields in all directions. In addition, the smart car learned from its experiences.

Experience is often more important than vision when it comes to safe driving. For example, it does not help to see a school bus if the driver does not also know that a school bus means kids are likely nearby, and the driver should expect lots of stops. As the Google cars drive around, their cameras and computers constantly record data. The car's AI technology identifies common obstacles, including pedestrians and other vehicles, and then creates models of these objects and their behavior.

For example, the car might record a person on a bicycle who stopped at a stop sign, stuck her arm out to the left side, and then turned left. Powerful

Mapping the World

The Google car does not rely on computer vision alone to know where it is going. Each car also has access to an incredibly detailed map. Researchers traveled the roads around Mountain View, California, where Google headquarters is located. They took precise measurements, including the position of every curb and the height of each traffic signal. They used this data to create a virtual world the cars use to navigate. As a Google car drives, it compares the data from its cameras and GPS to the data in the map to figure out where it is in space—with an accuracy of centimeters.

Google has completed these detailed measurements for approximately 2,000 miles (3,200 km) of roads in California. But in the United States alone, there are more than 4 million miles (6.4 million km) of roads.[5] To many, measuring all those roads would seem like an impossible project. But Google wants to make information about the real world accessible and searchable to cars, robots, and mobile devices. The company continues to work on the rest of the map.

The DARPA Challenge

Driverless car technology got off the ground in the deserts of California during a series of races that challenged engineers to push the limits of vehicle and AI technology. DARPA organized the first Grand Challenge in 2004 and offered a $1 million prize. The goal was to eventually develop vehicles to go into combat situations that are too dangerous for people. Not a single car completed the course in 2004. The next year, DARPA held the race again—this time for $2 million— and a team from Stanford University won with a robot car named Stanley.

computers at Google's headquarters churn through all this data and can eventually learn that a bicyclist who sticks out her arm to the left will turn left. Programmers do not have to add this knowledge manually. All of Google's cars connect to the same central "brain," so they can learn from each other's experiences. Each mile driven makes the entire fleet of vehicles smarter.

Connected Cars

In the future, all vehicles on the road may be able to talk to each other. The US Department of Transportation is working on vehicle-to-vehicle (V2V) communication. Cars that communicate with each other would provide several benefits.

To improve convenience, these cars could solve a problem many cities share: not enough parking. Larry Page of Google explained that a connected, driverless car could take passengers to work, drop them off at the door, and then go park somewhere out of the way. Later, "your phone notices that you're walking out of the building, and your car is there immediately by the time you get downstairs," said Page.[6]

Connected cars could constantly share information including the conditions of the road, traffic buildup, and other hazards. Sharing this information could significantly reduce the likelihood of

ANDROID

intel.

MDV

MOHR DAVIDOW VENTURES

VW

Red Bull

03

Drivers not required.

Can Humans Trust Driverless Cars?

Some people worry about what might happen if a driverless car's computers fail or experience a glitch. Another concern is hacking: someone could break into a car's computer to change its destination or cause an accident. Despite these issues, driverless cars are almost certainly safer than cars driven by people.

Car accidents are the leading cause of death for people under 34 in the United States, and nearly all of these accidents happen because a human being has made a mistake.[7] For example, a truck driver may have been distracted and missed seeing a bicyclist. Or a commuter running late for work may have gone through a red light.

AI technology cannot get distracted or feel rushed; it is entirely focused on the road and the obstacles around it. Sebastian Thrun of Stanford University, who helped develop the Google car, said, "I'm really looking forward to a time when generations after us look back at us and say how ridiculous it was that humans were driving cars."[8]

accidents. Traffic signals and road signs could become a thing of the past if cars could talk to each other and decide which one should go through an intersection first. These cars would also use much less gas because they would always choose the most efficient speeds and could plan their routes to prevent traffic jams.

Cars might even get to know their passengers. They could learn their owners' favorite music and restaurants, and they could connect to smartphones to help manage passengers' schedules or social networks. At some point, a car that could do all this might have to be called a robot.

A driver uses his smartphone to tell his car to find a parking spot.

SEVEN

ROBOTS
ON THE MOVE

DARPA's original series of races led to the first driverless cars. Then the agency challenged engineers once again. In 2012, DARPA offered a $2 million prize to the first team to build a robot that could drive a vehicle, walk across rubble, move debris, open a door, climb a ladder, break through concrete, replace a pump, and fix a leaking pipe. Existing robotics technology could accomplish any one of these tasks, but it is extremely difficult to design one robot that can complete all of them. Similar to other types of AI, robots tend to specialize in one particular thing. A robot may excel at navigating over rough terrain, but that same robot usually cannot climb a ladder or close a valve on a pipe. But soon this type of multipurpose bot may become common. Recent advances have led to robots that are better able to see, understand, and navigate the real world.

A robot called Valkyrie competes in the DARPA Robotics Challenge in 2013.

Mobility, Manipulation, and Messiness

The world is a confusing place to robots. According to Ken Goldberg of the University of California, Berkeley, this is how it would feel to be a robot today: "Everything is blurry and unsteady, low-resolution and jittery. . . . You can't perfectly control your own hands. It's like you're wearing huge oven mitts and goggles smeared with Vaseline."[1]

Rodney Brooks, a famous roboticist, sees three big problems facing robot technology: mobility, manipulation, and messiness. Mobility means getting around. Driverless car technology has solved many of the issues surrounding navigation and vision, but robots need to go places that cars cannot, such as up ladders and across rubble. Manipulation refers to what people do with their hands. Picking up a random object is a simple task for a human but extremely difficult for robots. If a robot grasps too hard, it could crush a plastic water bottle or a banana. But if it does not hold tightly enough, these same objects could fall out of its grip. Finally, messiness refers to the fact that the real world is full of surprises and unpredictability.

Baxter

Baxter, a robot produced by Rodney Brooks's company Rethink Robotics, marked a breakthrough in AI because of the way it interacts with people. Baxter is a stationary robot with long arms and pincer grips that can pick up, move, and manipulate objects. Robots with similar features already do many repetitive factory jobs. However, Baxter also has a face—two eyes on a computer screen that look in the direction in which it intends to move its arms. The robot also recognizes when its arms run into something unexpected, such as a person walking by, and will not try to push through. These two features make the robot much safer than current factory robots. Also, Baxter does not require special programming; instead, a factory worker can train the robot by moving its arms and showing it what to do.

Rodney **Brooks**
(1954–)

Rodney Brooks is not afraid of robots taking over the world. Instead, he worries that in the future, humans will not have enough robots. Brooks spent a decade directing the Artificial Intelligence Lab at MIT and has founded two robotics companies: iRobot and Rethink Robotics. The iRobot company sells the Roomba, a smart vacuum cleaner, and PackBot, a military robot that can defuse bombs. As a child growing up in Australia, Brooks built an electronic tic-tac-toe game and liked to make things explode.

In the 1980s, Brooks had a revolutionary idea that changed robotics. At the time, robots were big and slow. Brooks wondered why they were not more like insects—small in size but able to explore the environment on their own. He argued that robots should be "fast, cheap, and out of control."[2] Genghis, the buglike robot he built, could walk, climb over things, and follow people. This breakthrough inspired others to create robots with AI.

A team at the University of Maryland used deep learning techniques to teach the Baxter robot to perform cooking actions including cutting, stirring, and spreading. They trained the robot with a set of 88 videos taken from YouTube.[3] These videos contained extra data to label the objects and describe what is happening in each frame. One neural network in Baxter's AI system learned to identify objects in the videos, and another figured out the types of grasps the robot would need to use with those objects.

A worker at a plastics company performs his job alongside Baxter.

From these pieces, the AI system then created a vocabulary of actions and constructed a series of simple sentences to describe what the robot needed to do to accomplish the goals shown in the videos. Sentences included "grasp mustard," "grasp bread," and "action spread."[4] Yiannis Aloimonos, a computer science professor who helped train the robot, said: "Others have tried to copy the movements. Instead, we try to copy the goals. This is the breakthrough."[5]

Cloud Robotics

The most cutting-edge AI approaches to vision, learning, and decision-making take an incredible amount of computing power. One way to improve robots' intelligence is to connect them to the cloud. The cloud refers to powerful computers that devices connect to over the Internet. A robot can send data to a remote computer for high-speed processing and then receive instructions back. The powerful computer can act as a central "brain" for multiple robots that all share information and learn from each other.

Ken Goldberg's team built a cloud-based robot that can pick up different kinds of objects. It sends pictures from its cameras through a Google image search to find a match. Once it finds out what it is looking at—a bottle of mustard, for example—another program in the cloud matches the object to

a rough 3-D shape and suggests a series of motions to pick it up. The robot's AI looks at tens of thousands of different possibilities for the bottle's shape and position to determine the best action to take. Finally, the robot shares its knowledge. It uses sensors to create a 3-D model of the object, and it saves that information to the cloud, where other robots can learn from its experience.

DARPA engineer Brad Tousley, right, shows the Atlas robot to US Defense Secretary Chuck Hagel, left.

Robot Birds

A pigeon can outmaneuver a 747 jet. With this in mind, a team of roboticists at MIT set out to build a robot glider that could fly like a bird. In 2010, Russ Tedrake and his team demonstrated a glider that looks like a toy airplane but can swoop up to a wire, slow down, and land in a perch—just like a bird. Current flying robots, also known as unmanned aerial vehicles (UAVs), have to land on runways just like larger airplanes. The team used machine learning and trial and error to teach the glider. The next step will be to take their robot outside, where wind gusts and other "messiness" factors can cause problems. Eventually, the US Air Force hopes to use this technology to build UAVs that can recharge by perching on a wire.

Body Building

A humanlike brain is not the only thing people want from AI technology. People also expect robot bodies that can fluidly interact with the world. But a body is an incredibly complex thing. It took millions of years of evolution to produce the muscles and bones that propel humans and animals forward. Without flat, even surfaces, most walking robots tend to get stuck or fall over.

The company Boston Dynamics is working on solving this problem by giving its robots the ability to sense and adjust their balance continuously as they move around. Atlas, a robot that several teams are using in the DARPA challenge, can walk on a treadmill or over loose rubble. Boston Dynamics also produces a series of robots that are named after dogs: BigDog; AlphaDog; and the newest member of the family, Spot.

Spot can follow behind a human or robot leader across rough terrain, and it also has great balance. If the robot gets kicked, it can stay upright, and it can get up again on its own if it falls over.

Visitors to a military exposition look at one of the four-legged robots created by Boston Dynamics.

Hod Lipson of Cornell University uses computational evolution and robots to study movement. He hopes eventually to create a self-aware robot that can move on its own. In one experiment, the researchers simulated tissue, bone, and muscle in a computer program and then generated random combinations of those building blocks. Any combinations that helped the virtual robot move forward got to survive to the next round, which added more random mutations to the robots' bodies. After 1,000 generations, a few different ways for robots to move had evolved.[6] The researchers named them L-Walker, the Incher, the Push-Pull, the Jitter, the Jumper, and the Wings.

All of these different breakthroughs in robot motion allow machines to interact with the world more autonomously. More and more robots are able to operate without the need for a human controller.

ROBOTS TO THE RESCUE

A robot called DRC-HUBO turns a valve during the 2015 DARPA Robotics Challenge.

DARPA designed the Robotics Challenge after a 2011 earthquake and tsunami in Japan led to the Fukushima Daiichi nuclear disaster. The resulting radiation made the area unsafe for humans, which meant important repairs and other tasks could not be done. DARPA wants to inspire engineers to develop better, more independent, and more versatile robots that will be able to respond to challenging situations such as this.

In 2015, 25 teams competed in the DARPA Robotics Challenge Finals. In addition to completing many different types of tasks, each robot had to be battery powered (in case of a power failure during a disaster) and able to get up on its own if it fell over. Finally, the robots had to be autonomous—they had to be able to complete many of the tasks on their own, without people using remote controls to direct them. Here are a few of the contenders:

SCHAFT (GOOGLE)

This robot got the highest score in the tryouts for the challenge but dropped out of the competition afterward so the team could focus on creating a product for sale.

ROBOSIMIAN (NASA)

Similar to an ape, this robot uses all four arms and legs to complete tasks.

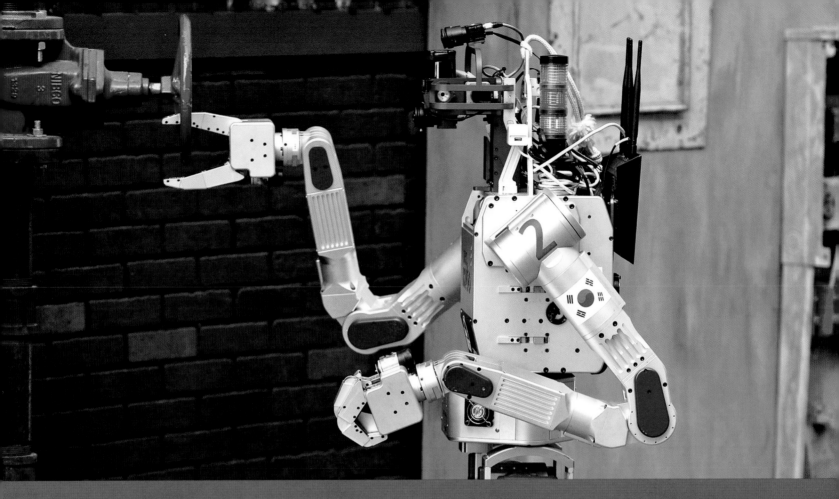

TARTAN RESCUE CHIMP (CARNEGIE MELLON UNIVERSITY)

Four tank-like treads on its arms and feet allow this robot to switch from driving around to standing and using its

three-fingered, pincerlike hands.

DRC-HUBO (TEAM KAIST)

This robot, which won the 2015 competition, was made by a team from South Korea.

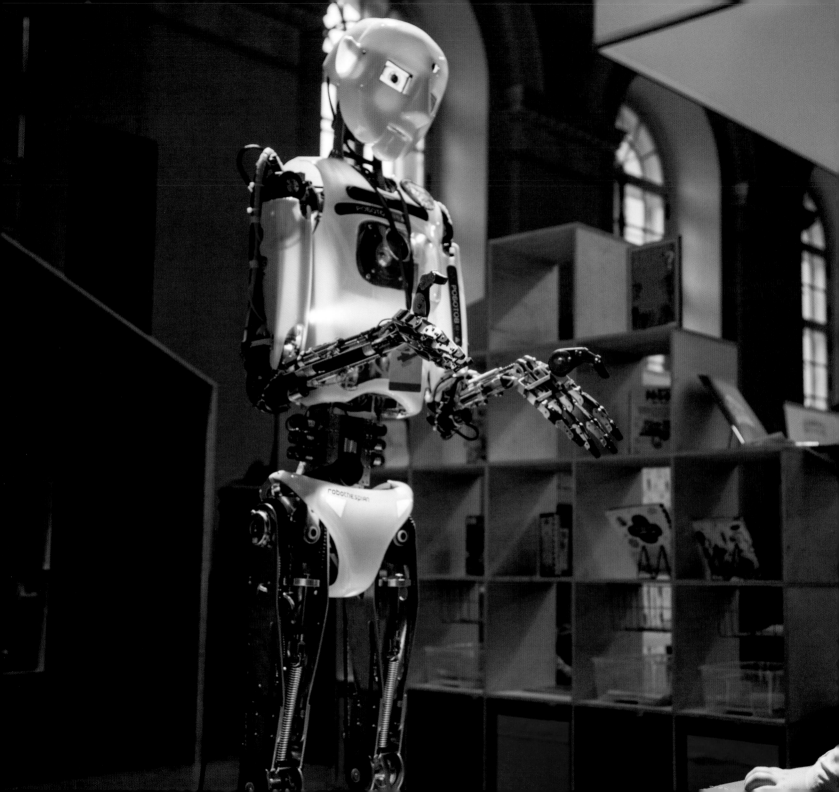

EIGHT

ROBOT COMPANIONS AND ARTISTS

In popular culture and science fiction, robots are often depicted as brutal metal soldiers that follow instructions precisely with no regard for human life or human feelings. And it is true that many advances in AI and robotics do not bother with creativity, emotions, or social behavior. But some researchers are working on friendly AI technology that can maintain a close connection with human companions while providing people with advanced knowledge or an extra set of hands. Social robots already help entertain families, keep astronauts company in space, and care for the elderly. Robot artists paint, make music, and write stories.

A robot interacts with a child at a technology conference in Moscow, Russia.

A Global Brain

When the virtual assistant Siri was in development, its creators wanted to give the app some personality, so they spent time brainstorming snarky comebacks to some of the questions people might ask. However, these responses were all preprogrammed— Siri did not come up with them on its own. The next generation of virtual assistants will be much smarter and more autonomous.

The creators of Siri have a new project named Viv. Dag Kittlaus, an entrepreneur on the team, said: "Boy, wouldn't it be nice if you could talk to everything, and it knew you, and it knew everything about you, and it could do everything?" This grand vision of a "global brain" is what the team has in mind for Viv. They want to make intelligence into a utility that anyone can tap into, similar to electricity or wireless Internet. Current virtual assistants, including Siri, Cortana, and Google Now, are all tied to a particular platform and company. The team working on Viv hopes it will interface with every type of mobile device.

Viv will also be able to respond to much more complex questions and requests. Siri, for example, can answer simple knowledge questions or handle basic requests such as "Where is Grand Central Station?" or "What is the closest Chinese restaurant?" But more complicated questions with several

A nursing home resident in Japan interacts with a Paro robot.

◢ Caring for Grandma

By 2050, 16 percent of the global population will be over 65 years old.[1] These elderly men and women will need extra care, but there may not be enough human nurses to go around. Instead, the elderly could rely on robots. Some will help monitor people's health or assist with daily routines. Robear is a large, friendly-looking robot with long arms that can help people turn over, stand, or get out of bed and into a chair. Other robots will provide company or even conversation. Some nursing homes in Japan already use the Paro therapy bot, which looks like a baby seal and reacts to voices and touch. The same company also released the Palro, a small humanoid robot that talks and plays games.

The Kismet robot demonstrates
one of its facial expressions
for Breazeal.

Rapping Robot

After building a desk lamp robot, Guy Hoffman went on to develop a robot musician that could play and improvise alongside people. It uses mallets to play the marimba, and its AI programming allows it to create music as well as listen and respond to human players. Hoffman realized the robot also needed a way to express itself, so he built a head for the robot that bobs in time with the music and turns toward the other players when it is ready for them to join in. Hoffman even invited a rapper to jam with the robot, and the rapper soon started bobbing his head along with the machine.

Guy Hoffman of MIT studies interactions and teamwork between humans and robots, and he has worked with Breazeal at the MIT media lab. Before he started building robots, Hoffman studied animation, which is where he learned that emotion is expressed in body movements. A talented animator can make even a cartoon piece of furniture seem alive. Hoffman decided to try to re-create this idea with a robot built to look like a desk lamp. He wrote two different AI programs for the lamp-shaped robot. One program calculated everything the robot had to do, like a traditional robot. The other used embodied artificial intelligence, or learning through body motions, and it mimicked actions and sometimes took chances by making a decision to move without calculating first. In separate tests, Hoffman had groups of volunteers interact with the different systems. People who met the more adventurous robot called it "he" or "she" and even said they felt like "good friends" with it.[3] Nobody said that about the more calculating robot. The abilities to mimic actions and take risks made the robot seem like it had a personality.

One place where humans could use robot friends is in outer space. Robots are always helpful on space missions because they can accomplish tasks that are difficult, dangerous, or boring for humans. NASA developed Robonaut for this purpose. But loneliness also takes a toll during a long stay at the

Fuminori Kataoka, an engineer at Toyota, has a conversation with Kirobo.

International Space Station (ISS). Kirobo, a doll-sized robot with cartoony features, became the first companion robot to travel to space in August 2013. It could understand and speak Japanese thanks to language processing AI, and it could recognize faces and emotions. Kirobo's purpose during its 18-month stay on the ISS was to keep astronauts company.

Creative AI

Angelina, the AI program that makes its own video games, is not the only computer that can create something new. Researchers have built AI programs that generate their own original music, paintings, and stories. This type of AI is called computational creativity, and many of these programs actually help human artists be more creative. For example, the What-if Machine generates combinations of ideas that a human writer could use as inspiration. People who try out the What-if Machine can grade the results, teaching the AI to generate better ideas next time. Other AI artists' work can stand on its own. For example, computer programs have produced music albums and exhibited in art galleries.

Iamus is a program that composes original music. Researchers at the University of Malaga in Spain taught Iamus musical composition rules and used an evolutionary algorithm to allow the AI to experiment with different approaches. The AI writes a set of random songs based on the rules and then evaluates the results and chooses the best ones. These songs are then mutated, and the AI picks out the best results, repeating this process again and again until it achieves a finished song. Unlike earlier music-generating AI, which imitated the styles of human composers, Iamus was able to develop its own style. The more Iamus creates, the more polished its music sounds.

Simon Colton of the University of London created an AI program called the Painting Fool that produces artwork. He hopes people will come to appreciate the computer program as an artist on its own and not simply as the tool of a human creator. However, many argue the actual artist is the human who created the AI program.

Creative AI can help advance the sciences, too. Adam is a computer program that made a splash in 2009 when it designed and carried out its own science experiments—as many as 1,000 each day—and became the first machine to discover new knowledge on its own.[4] Now, the same research group has

The Painting Fool

The Painting Fool uses several different creative processes to create artwork. To turn a news article into a collage, it uses keywords from the article to search for pictures on the web, and then it interprets the images and combines them together. It can also use machine vision to detect emotions in people and then paint their portraits in styles that match their moods. In a 2013 exhibit in Paris, France, titled *You Can't Know My Mind*, the program analyzed random news articles for emotional words, and its own mood changed to one of six states based on what it had read: very happy, happy, experimental, reflexive, sad, and very sad. People could ask the Painting Fool to paint their portraits, and the computer's mood would influence the result. When it was very sad, it refused to paint at all.

developed Eve, an AI program that will work on discovering new drugs.

Companion robots and creative AI programs can express emotions through their voices, body motions, or artwork, but whether the program actually experiences emotions is open for debate. Most people argue that a computer cannot experience feelings. They say there is no "self" inside the machine that understands what it means to be happy, sad, surprised, or angry. This may be true, but as AI becomes more complex and more autonomous, it may become hard to explain away the possibility that computers can have conscious selves just like people.

This piece of art was created by the Painting Fool.

NINE

THE FUTURE OF AI

AI technology connects people to information instantly, solves difficult problems, expands human knowledge and creativity, and even entertains people or keeps them company. But AI also has the potential to go terribly wrong. Popular movies show what might happen if robots or computer programs turn against their human creators. In the 1999 movie *The Matrix*, robots have enslaved humans in virtual reality, and in the 1968 movie *2001: A Space Odyssey*, a computer called HAL 9000 causes the deaths of almost all of the crew members on a spaceship.

Could intelligent computers or robots actually take over the world? Some people worry this is a real possibility. Right now, all AI technology is considered weak AI, or AI that solves a specific problem or performs a certain duty such as language processing or image recognition. In contrast, strong AI is a single

A robot called Pepper was designed to understand human emotions.

computer or robot that can perform a full range of intelligent tasks on its own. The possibility that humans could lose control over AI scares some experts.

Renowned physicist Stephen Hawking spoke out about the potential dangers in 2014: "One can imagine such technology outsmarting financial markets, out-inventing human researchers, out-manipulating human leaders, and developing weapons we cannot even understand," he said.[1] To avoid these problems, humans need to make sure they stay in control of AI technology. In 2015, AI experts—including the team that built Watson and the founders of the company Deep Mind—signed a letter promising to protect humanity from machines. The letter included guidelines for safe AI development.

◢ Equal Rights for AI

As computers and robots get smarter and smarter, many people are starting to ask whether they deserve equal rights. Scientists and philosophers have been wondering about this since the early days of computing. Some say the question is meaningless because there is no reason to program AI technology with abilities and feelings similar to those of humans. They argue that it makes more sense to build AI that performs with better-than-human ability at a particular task. In fact, they say AI consciousness could get in the way. For example, an AI that is supposed to be flying an airplane may get bored and decide to write a song instead. Therefore, they say, it does not make sense for airplane-flying AI to even have the ability to understand music.

Brain Chips and Quantum Computers

AI is limited by the speed of computers. The layered neural networks that make deep learning possible require a huge amount of computer processing time and power. When the Google Brain group ran the program that discovered cats on YouTube in 2012, 1,000 computers needed three days to process the information because the neural network was so massive, with 1 billion connections.[2]

Since then, researchers have been programming even larger, more complex neural networks, but computer hardware has limited how well and how fast these networks can perform. A type of processor called a neuromorphic chip could change everything. Instead of programming software to simulate a neural network, researchers can use these chips to achieve the same results. IBM's TrueNorth neuromorphic chip comes with a network that has 1 million neurons and 256 million connections between them.[3] If researchers need a bigger network than that, they can link several of the chips together. These chips require much less energy than normal, mostly because they run only when they need to. In contrast, regular processors are always running. Neuromorphic chips could potentially bring powerful AI to mobile devices without draining the battery.

Quantum computing is another approach that could offer increased processing speed to help power AI technology. Google and NASA launched a Quantum Artificial Intelligence Lab in 2013, and they have already developed machine-learning techniques using the futuristic computer. However, this technology is far from being practically useful.

The Internet of Things

Once advanced AI technology gets fast enough and efficient enough, people could start to see everyday objects get smarter, including kitchen appliances, cars, and even clothing. The Nest Learning Thermostat, for example, automatically adjusts a home's temperature after learning when the people in that particular home want it warm or cool.

Quantum AI

A regular computer stores information in its memory as bits. A bit can have one of two values: 0 or 1. A quantum computer uses qubits, which can also hold information that is in both states at once. This type of computing can speed up processing for many applications, including AI.

Quantum computers exist but are not yet ready for everyday use. The one at the Quantum Artificial Intelligence Lab must be kept extremely cold—colder than interstellar space. Although the computer itself is not huge, the machines that keep it cold take up most of a room. The lab has written machine learning programs to run on this computer.

The concept of an Internet of Things has been around for years, and it is just starting to become reality. It is the idea that the objects people own and use every day will gather data and then share that information through connections to the cloud or to other objects. The more information gets shared, the more data will be available to AI systems, and the smarter they will get.

Cheaper sensor technology makes the Internet of Things possible. Sensors that detect temperature, position, and people's faces will be able to constantly observe the world. This will give people access to

Am I a Robot?

Rodney Brooks believes humans are already robots. "I, you, our family, friends, and dogs—we all are machines," he wrote.[4] According to Brooks and many other scientists and philosophers, human minds and bodies work because of the way the billions of molecules interact. According to this view, a person's feelings and sense of self are the result of patterns of reactions inside the brain and could not exist separately from the brain. This way of thinking means if humans learn the rules that make the brain work, they could re-create it in robots or computers. Brooks said, "I believe our creation would exhibit genuine human-level intelligence, emotions, and even consciousness."[5]

much more data than ever before, in real time. Artificial intelligence systems, such as Viv, will analyze this data and use it to accomplish tasks, learn, and communicate with people. For example, sensors in a farmer's field could monitor the soil and weather, giving an AI system the data it needs to determine the best time to water or fertilize the crops. Eventually, all devices could learn to know what people need and want before they even ask.

In the future, children may get ready to leave for school and have a car pull up to their home automatically. The car arrives on its own, because it knows the children always leave at that time. Around lunchtime, before the children are even hungry, a device in their eyeglasses may suggest a few meal options and then automatically place an order for them. Later, a child may start to feel sick to her stomach. Tiny robots inside her bloodstream may send information about her internal systems to a medical AI. The AI would then analyze the child's symptoms and determine an appropriate treatment.

Merging with Computers

As computer systems learn to understand and interact with the real world in the Internet of Things, humans will also spend more and more of their time in the virtual world. Cynthia Breazeal is

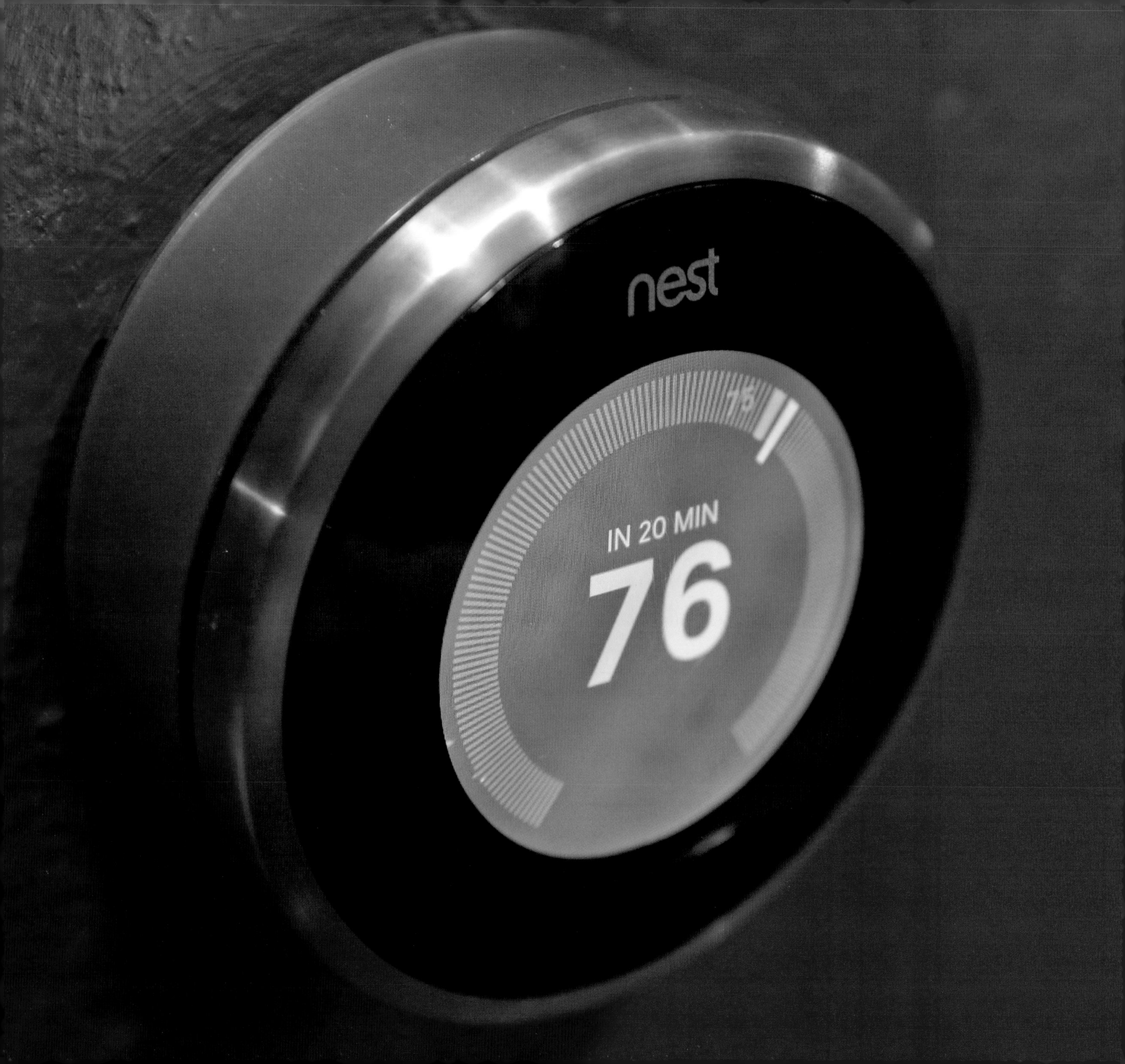
nest
IN 20 MIN
76
75

experimenting with "mixed reality," or virtual games and stories with content that can come to life. Some experts, including Ray Kurzweil, believe the digital and physical worlds will merge so completely that humans and computers will effectively become one. He predicts that tiny robots inside our bodies will monitor health, mood, and other physical processes.

Many people already post information about themselves on social media and record videos of their lives. Wearable devices that track motion will only add to this heap of virtual personal information. The more data that exists about people online, the more they become virtual beings. At some future date, it may even be possible to create a virtual self from a digitized copy of a person's brain. In essence, a human being could become a computer program.

At the same time, AI will enhance the way people think, reason, create, and move in the real world. Today, people already use smartphones and computers to help get directions, remember facts and names, and organize their daily lives. In the future, humans will depend on these devices even more—to solve problems and keep people company. Robots will also become a bigger part of daily life. They will cook and clean, manufacture items people need, and

◂ Mixed Reality

Cynthia Breazeal has built robots that exist in mixed reality, or in both the real world and a virtual world. For example, a child may watch a robot wandering around on a large computer screen. Then, a door opens up at the base of the wall, and the robot walks out. After the robot emerges into the real world, the child can talk to it or play with it. Any changes that take place will transfer back to the robot's virtual counterpart. For example, if a child changes the letter displaying on the robot's chest, the same letter will show up on the virtual robot when it goes back through the door and reappears on the screen. This type of technology would allow kids (or adults) to actively participate in a story, movie, or video game.

perform surgeries. Artificial intelligence will become more normal and more human. One day, it might not be strange for a person to say a robot or virtual assistant is her best friend.

A robot known as PR2 can perform household tasks such as cooking.

ESSENTIAL FACTS

Key Discoveries

» **Deep learning:** This technique allows computers to learn to recognize patterns, such as the sounds that make up words or the shapes that make up a human face. It is inspired by the neural network inside the brain.

» **Driverless cars:** The Google driverless car has traveled more than 1 million miles (1.6 million km) on regular roads without causing any accidents. The car uses sensors and AI to orient itself on the road and to detect and avoid obstacles.

» **Virtual assistant:** Apple devices come with a virtual assistant named Siri who can respond to certain voice commands and answer questions. Siri's competition includes Microsoft's Cortana, Google Now, and Amazon's Echo. Siri's creators are working on an even smarter assistant named Viv.

Key Players

» **Google:** Sebastian Thrun works on the Google driverless car, Geoffrey Hinton and Andrew Ng contribute to deep learning research, and Ray Kurzweil works on natural language processing. Google purchased the AI company Deep Mind in 2014.

» **IBM:** Researchers at IBM built Watson, an AI program that defeated human opponents on *Jeopardy!* in 2011.

» **Massachusetts Institute of Technology (MIT):** Rodney Brooks heads up the MIT artificial intelligence lab and founded two robotics companies. At the MIT media lab, Cynthia Breazeal directs the personal robotics group.

Key Tools and Technologies

» **Neural networks:** Neural networks can process huge amounts of data to find patterns that combine into higher and higher levels of meaning. The technique is inspired by the network inside the human brain.

» **Robotics:** In the field of robotics, AI technology provides tools to see, understand, and navigate the real world. Researchers have developed robots that learn to use their bodies and other senses through trial and error.

» **Speech recognition:** Speech recognition allows AI technology to respond to voice commands or transcribe spoken sentences. This technology has improved dramatically since 2010 with the help of deep learning algorithms.

Future Outlook

Some experts worry humans could lose control over AI technology if computers or robots ever start to think for themselves. Others believe AI will always be programmed to meet a specific need and will not gain consciousness. Either way, over the next decade, sensors and devices will gather more and more data, which will feed into smarter AI systems that learn to understand human behavior and anticipate people's needs. Cars will drive themselves, mobile devices will learn people's daily routines, and it will not seem strange to talk to a computer.

Quote

"We want to take AI . . . to wonderful new places, where no person, no student, no program has gone before."

—*Geoffrey Hinton, Distinguished Professor, University of Toronto*

GLOSSARY

adaptive cruise control

A system that enables a car to drive on its own, with a human driver available to take over if needed.

autonomous

Able to act without help or direction.

binary code

A series of ones and zeros that a computer reads in order to run a program.

computational evolution

A computer simulation that generates random combinations of elements, chooses the best results, and repeats the process again and again.

computer vision

The ability of computers or robots to detect images with the help of cameras and programs.

Defense Advanced Research Projects Agency (DARPA)

An agency of the US military that provides money and sponsors contests to help develop new technology.

facial recognition

The ability of computers or robots to identify people in images.

finite state machine

A technique used to model behavior. The state machine stores each state separately along with instructions on how to transition between states.

neural network

A group of interconnected neurons. The brain is a neural network, and simulations of this type of network are important for AI.

neuromorphic chip

A computer chip that processes information using neural networks.

neuron

A brain cell that sends electric signals.

non-player character

Any video game character that behaves automatically and is not controlled by a human.

pathfinding

The ability to navigate between two points.

procedural generation

The use of a program to automatically create content.

programmer

A person who writes coded instructions for a computer.

prototype

An initial sample of a product idea.

speech recognition

The ability of computers or robots to detect spoken words.

vehicle-to-vehicle communication

The ability of two cars to share information.

ADDITIONAL RESOURCES

Selected Bibliography

Henig, Robin Marantz. "The Real Transformers." *New York Times*. New York Times Company, 29 Jul. 2007. Web. 29 Apr. 2015.

Howard, Jeremy. "The Wonderful and Terrifying Implications of Computers that Can Learn." *TED*. TED Conferences, Dec. 2014. Web. 17 Aug. 2015.

Jones, Nicola. "Computer Science: The Learning Machines." *Nature*. Nature Publishing Group, 8 Jan. 2014. Web. 29 Apr. 2015.

Kelly, Kevin. "The Three Breakthroughs that Have Finally Unleashed AI on the World." *Wired*. Condé Nast, 27 Oct. 2014. Web. 29 Apr. 2015.

Further Readings

Bueno, Carlos. *Lauren Ipsum: A Story about Computer Science and Other Improbable Things*. San Francisco: No Starch, 2015. Print.

Foran, Racquel. *Robotics: From Automatons to the Roomba*. Minneapolis: Abdo, 2015. Print.

Hamen, Susan E. *Google: The Company and Its Founders*. Minneapolis: Abdo, 2011. Print.

Websites

To learn more about Cutting-Edge Science and Technology, visit **booklinks.abdopublishing.com**. These links are routinely monitored and updated to provide the most current information available.

For More Information

For more information on this subject, contact or visit the following organizations:

Association for the Advancement of Artificial Intelligence (AAAI)
2275 East Bayshore Road, Suite 160
Palo Alto, California 94303
650-328-3123
http://www.aaai.org/

This nonprofit society sponsors conferences and awards to promote the development of AI technology.

FIRST (For Inspiration and Recognition of Science and Technology)
200 Bedford Street
Manchester, NH 03101
603-666-3906
http://www.usfirst.org/

Founded by inventor Dean Kamen, the FIRST Robotics Competition challenges students to build and program robots. Teams learn about real-world science, technology, and engineering.

MIT Media Lab
77 Massachusetts Avenue, E14/E15
Cambridge, MA 02139
617-253-5960
http://www.media.mit.edu/

Researchers at the MIT Media Lab study the use of digital technologies and how they can help us think, express, communicate, and explore.

SOURCE NOTES

Chapter 1. Computer Champions

1. Chante Smith. "Jeopardy (February 14, 2011) IBM Challenge Day 1." Online video clip. *Dailymotion*. Dailymotion, 14 Feb. 2011. Web. 14 July 2015.

2. Ben Cosman. "Ken Jennings, Brad Rutter, and What It's Like to Be the Best Ever on 'Jeopardy!'" The Wire. The Atlantic Monthly Group, 15 May 2014. Web. 14 July 2015.

3. "About IBM Watson Fact Sheet." *IBM*. IBM, n.d. Web. 14 July 2015.

4. Evan Moore. "For Watson, Jeopardy! Is Elementary." *The Tech*. The Tech, 18 Feb. 2011. Web. 14 July 2015.

5. John Markoff. "Computer Wins on 'Jeopardy!': Trivial, It's Not." *New York Times*. New York Times Company, 16 Feb. 2011. Web. 14 July 2015.

6. Monty Newborn. *Deep Blue: An Artificial Intelligence Milestone*. New York: Springer, 2003. Print. 10–11.

7. "Kasparov vs Deep Blue: A Contrast in Styles." *IBM*. IBM, n.d. Web. 14 July 2015.

8. Geoff Brumfiel. "Look Out, This Poker-Playing Computer Is Unbeatable." NPR. NPR, 8 Jan. 2015. Web. 14 July 2015.

Chapter 2. Deep Learning

1. Carl Zimmer. "100 Trillion Connections: New Efforts Probe and Map the Brain's Detailed Architecture." *Scientific American*. Scientific American, Jan. 2011. Web. 14 July 2015.

2. Joyce Noah-Vanhoucke. "Merck Competition Results - Deep NN and GPUs Come Out to Play." *Kaggle*. Kaggle, 31 Oct. 2012. Web. 14 July 2015.

3. Nicola Jones. "Computer Science: The Learning Machines." *Nature*. Nature Publishing Group, 8 Jan. 2014. Web. 14 July 2015.

4. Daniela Hernandez. "Meet the Man Google Hired to Make AI a Reality." *Wired*. Condé Nast, 16 Jan. 2014. Web. 14 July 2015.

5. Andrew Nusca. "The 'Largest AI Program in History' Led to Apple's Siri." *ZDNet*. CBS Interactive, 23 Jan. 2013. Web. 14 July 2015.

6. Nicola Jones. "Computer Science: The Learning Machines." *Nature*. Nature Publishing Group, 8 Jan. 2014. Web. 14 July 2015.

7. Dharshan Kumaran and Demis Hassabis. "From Pixels to Actions: Human-Level Control through Deep Reinforcement Learning." *Google Research Blog*. Google, 25 Feb. 2015. Web. 14 July 2015.

8. Larry Page. "Where's Google Going Next?" *TED*. TED Conferences, Mar. 2014. Web. 17 Aug. 2015.

Chapter 3. Got the Picture?

1. "Are You a Robot? Introducing 'No CAPTCHA reCAPTCHA.'" *Google Online Security Blog*. Google, 3 Dec. 2014. Web. 14 July 2015.

2. Kaiming He, Xiangyu Zhang, Shaoqing Ren, and Jian Sun. "Delving Deep into Rectifiers: Surpassing Human-Level Performance on ImageNet Classification." *arXiv*. Cornell University Library, 6 Feb. 2015. Web. 14 July 2015.

3. "How Google Cracked House Number Identification in Street View." *MIT Technology Review*. MIT Technology Review, 6 Jan. 2014. Web. 14 July 2015.

4. John Markoff. "Computer Eyesight Gets a Lot More Accurate." *New York Times*. New York Times Company, 18 Aug. 2014. Web. 14 July 2015.

5. "Large Scale Visual Recognition Challenge 2010 (ILSVRC2010)." *Imagenet*. Stanford Vision Lab, Stanford University, Princeton University, n.d. Web. 14 July 2015.

6. Andrej Karpathy and Li Fei-Fei. "Deep Visual-Semantic Alignments for Generating Image Descriptions." *Stanford Vision Lab*. Stanford University, n.d. Web. 14 July 2015.

7. John Bohannon. "Facebook Will Soon Be Able to ID You in Any Photo." *Science Magazine*. American Association for the Advancement of Science, 5 Feb. 2015. Web. 14 July 2015.

8. Yaniv Taigman, et. al. "DeepFace: Closing the Gap to Human-Level Performance in Face Verification." *IEEE Xplore*. IEEE, n.d. Web. 14 July 2015.

9. "Single Page of All Names (No Thumbnails)." *Labeled Faces in the Wild*. University of Massachusetts Amherst, n.d. Web. 14 July 2015.

10. Tom Simonite. "Facebook Creates Software That Matches Faces Almost as Well as You Do." *MIT Technology Review*. MIT Technology Review, 17 Mar. 2014. Web. 14 July 2015.

11. Chaochao Lu and Xiaoou Tang. "Surpassing Human-Level Face Verification Performance on LFW with GaussianFace." *arXiv*. Cornell University Library, 20 Dec. 2014. Web. 14 July 2015.

12. John Bohannon. "Facebook Will Soon Be Able to ID You in Any Photo." *Science Magazine*. American Association for the Advancement of Science, 5 Feb. 2015. Web. 14 July 2015.

13. Renee Lewis. "FBI Rolls Out New Facial Recognition Program." *Al Jazeera America*. Al Jazeera America, 15 Sep. 2014. Web. 14 July 2015.

Chapter 4. Talking with Machines

1. Marvin L. Minsky. "Future of AI Technology." *MIT Media Lab*. MIT Media Lab, 2 Jan. 1997. Web. 14 July 2015.

2. Robert Hof. "Interview: How Ray Kurzweil Plans to Revolutionize Search at Google." *Forbes*. Forbes, 29 Apr. 2013. Web. 14 July 2015.

3. Elise Ackerman. "Google Now Scores Higher than Siri and Cortana on Massive Knowledge Quiz. An AI Breakthrough? Not So Fast." *Forbes*. Forbes, 10 Oct. 2014. Web. 14 July 2015.

4. A. M. Turing. "Computing Machinery and Intelligence." *Mind* 59.236 (1950): 433–460. *JSTOR*, n.d. Web. 14 July 2015.

5. Ibid.

SOURCE NOTES CONTINUED

6. Andrew Griffin. "Turing Test Breakthrough as Super-Computer Becomes First to Convince Us It's Human." *The Independent*. The Independent, 8 June 2014. Web. 14 July 2015.

7. David Auerbach. "A Computer Program Finally Passed the Turing Test?" *Bitwise*. The Slate Group, 10 June 2014. Web. 14 July 2015.

8. B. Jack Copeland and Diane Proudfoot. "Alan Turing: Father of the Modern Computer." *Rutherford Journal*. Rutherford Journal, n.d. Web. 14 July 2015.

9. Robert Hof. "Baidu Announces Breakthrough in Speech Recognition, Claiming to Top Google and Apple." *Forbes*. Forbes, 18 Dec. 2014. Web. 14 July 2015.

10. Derrik Harris. "Baidu Claims Deep Learning Breakthrough with Deep Speech." *Gigaom*. Knowingly, Inc., 18 Dec. 2014. Web. 14 July 2015.

11. Robert Hof. "Baidu Announces Breakthrough in Speech Recognition, Claiming to Top Google and Apple." *Forbes*. Forbes, 18 Dec. 2014. Web. 14 July 2015.

12. Derrik Harris. "Baidu Claims Deep Learning Breakthrough with Deep Speech." *Gigaom*. Knowingly, Inc., 18 Dec. 2014. Web. 14 July 2015.

13. Jack Clark. "Speech Recognition Better Than a Human's Exists. You Just Can't Use It Yet." *Bloomberg Business*. Bloomberg, 23 Dec. 2014. Web. 14 July 2015.

14. Michael Keller. "Microsoft Rebuilding Babel." *Txchnologist*. General Electric, 9 Nov. 2012. Web. 14 July 2015.

Chapter 5. Video Games

1. Damian Isla. Personal interview. 8 Jan. 2015.

2. Michael Cook. Personal Interview. 8 Apr. 2015.

Chapter 6. Driverless Cars

1. Jeremy Howard. "The Wonderful and Terrifying Implications of Computers That Can Learn." *TED*. TED Conferences, Dec. 2014. Web. 17 Aug. 2015.

2. Bill Howard. "What Is Adaptive Cruise Control, and How Does It Work?" *ExtremeTech*. Ziff Davis, 4 June 2013. Web. 14 July 2015.

3. "Cars Can Brake for Pedestrians if Drivers Don't." *IIHS*. IIHS, 30 Mar. 2011. Web. 14 July 2015.

4. John Markoff. "Google's Next Phase in Driverless Cars: No Steering Wheel or Brake Pedals." *New York Times*. New York Times Company, 27 May 2014. Web. 14 July 2015.

5. Alexis C. Madrigal. "The Trick That Makes Google's Self-Driving Cars Work." *Atlantic*. Atlantic Monthly Group, 15 May 2014. Web. 14 July 2015.

6. Miguel Helft. "The Future According to Google's Larry Page." *Fortune*. Time, Inc., 3 Jan. 2013. Web. 14 July 2015.

7. Larry Page. "Where's Google Going Next?" *TED*. TED Conferences, Mar. 2014. Web. 17 Aug. 2015.

8. Sebastian Thrun. "Google's Driverless Car." *TED*. TED Conferences, Mar. 2011. Web. 17 Aug. 2015.

Chapter 7. Robots on the Move

1. Thu-Huang Ha. "The Surprising Thing Robots Can't Do Yet: Housework." *TED*. TED Conferences, 2 Oct. 2014. Web. 14 July 2015.

2. Rodney A. Brooks and Anita M. Flynn. "Fast, Cheap and Out of Control: A Robot Invasion of the Solar System." *Journal of the British Interplanetary Society* 42 (1989): 478–485. *MIT*, n.d. Web. 14 July 2015.

3. Yezhou Yang, Yi Li, Cornelia Fermüller, and Yiannis Aloimonos. "Robot Learning Manipulation Action Plans by 'Watching' Unconstrained Videos from the World Wide Web." *University of Maryland Institute for Advanced Computer Studies.* University of Maryland, n.d. Web. 14 July 2015.

4. Ibid.

5. "Robots Learn to Use Kitchen Tools by Watching YouTube Videos." *University of Maryland*. University of Maryland, 12 Jan. 2015. Web. 14 July 2015.

6. Wynne Parry. "Evolution Helps Build Better Robots." *Discovery News*. Discovery Communications, 22 May 2013. Web. 14 July 2015.

7. Hod Lipson. "Building 'Self-Aware' Robots." *TED*. TED Conferences, Mar. 2007. Web. 17 Aug. 2015.

Chapter 8. Robot Companions and Artists

1. Heather Kelly. "Robots: The Future of Elder Care?" *CNN*. Cable News Network, Inc., 19 July 2013. Web. 14 July 2015.

2. James Temple. "Boston Researcher Cynthia Breazeal Is Ready to Bring Robots into the Home. Are You?" *Re/Code*. Revere Digital, 12 Dec. 2014. Web. 14 July 2015.

3. Guy Hoffman. "Robots with 'Soul.'" *TED*. TED Conferences, Oct. 2013. Web. 17 Aug. 2015.

4. Lizzie Buchen. "Robot Makes Scientific Discovery All by Itself." *Wired*. Condé Nast, 2 Apr. 2009. Web. 14 July 2015.

Chapter 9. The Future of AI

1. Stephen Hawking, Stuart Russell, Max Tegmark, and Frank Wilczek. "Stephen Hawking: 'Transcendence Looks at the Implications of Artificial Intelligence - But Are We Taking AI Seriously Enough?'" *The Independent*. The Independent, 1 May 2014. Web. 14 July 2015.

2. "Google Computer Works Out How to Spot Cats." *BBC*. BBC, 26 June 2012. Web. 14 July 2015.

3. "Brain Power." *IBM Research*. IBM, n.d. Web. 14 July 2015.

4. Rodney Brooks. "I, Rodney Brooks, Am a Robot." *IEEE Spectrum*. IEEE, 1 June 2008. Web. 14 July 2015.

5. Ibid.

INDEX

About the Author

Kathryn Hulick lives in Massachusetts with her family. Her husband, Steve Gargolinski, worked as an AI programmer on video games and gave her lots of great ideas for this book. They like to hike, read, visit the ocean, and play with their dog, Maya. They welcomed their first baby, Seth, in 2014. Kathryn has always been fascinated by the idea that computers and robots could learn how to think and feel.